Willie Mosconi's
WINNING
POCKET
BILLIARDS

Author of

Willie Mosconi on Pocket Billiards

Willie Mosconi's
WINNING
POCKET
BILLIARDS

For Beginners
and Advanced Players
With a Section on Trick Shots
By Willie Mosconi

Crown Trade Paperbacks
New York

Published by Crown Trade Paperbacks, 201 East 50th Street, New York, New York 10022.
Member of the Crown Publishing Group.

Originally published in paperback by Crown Publishers, Inc., in 1965.

Random House, Inc. New York, Toronto, London, Sydney, Auckland

Crown Trade Paperbacks and colophon are trademarks of Crown Publishers, Inc.

Manufactured in the United States of America

Library of Congress Catalog Card Number: 65-15836

ISBN 0-517-88427-5

10 9 8 7 6 5 4 3 2 1

First Crown Trade Paperbacks Edition

To the women in my life—Flora, my wife, and my daughters Candace and Gloria—I lovingly dedicate this book.

Contents

Foreword
by Stanley Cohen

Tribute To A Champion

> It's a great feeling, boy, it's a great feeling when
> you're right and you know you're right . . . You make
> shots that nobody's ever made before. And you play
> the game the way nobody's ever played it before."

— FROM THE MOVIE *THE HUSTLER*

Willie Mosconi played pocket billiards the way nobody ever
played it before. He had embraced the game as if by birthright and
played it with the simmering elegance of a virtuoso who understood
its simple truth right from the start. For more than half a century —
from the time he won his first world championship in 1941 until his
death in 1993 — the name Willie Mosconi has been part of the lex-
icon of American sports. Even those who had never hefted a pool
cue or seen a game knew that "Mosconi" meant pocket billiards, or
pool as it was more commonly called. He achieved a level of fame
that few men ever know: His name had become synonymous with
his occupation.

Willie was literally born into the game, courtesy of his father,
Joseph William Mosconi, a professional prizefighter who never
quite made it to the top. When his career as a bantamweight was
over, the elder Mosconi opened a small, five-table pool hall in South
Philadelphia. The family lived in rooms on the floor above, and
young Willie, then six years old, was attracted by the sight and

sound of brightly colored balls flashing across the green felt table. His father, however, was determined that his son would have no part of either boxing or billiards. By paternal edict, the pool hall was placed off-limits. But the youngster was not easily discouraged. Destiny, it might be said, was on his side.

At night, Willie sometimes climbed down the rainpipe from his room and entered the pool hall through a rear window. His father responded by locking up the balls and cue sticks at the end of the day's business. Willie was forced to improvise. He went to the pantry, selected the roundest small potatoes he could find, used a broom handle as a cue stick, and knocked the potatoes around the table while standing atop an apple crate. But his father was adamant. He had already chosen a career for his son and was intent upon steering him in that direction. He wanted Willie to be a dancer.

It was not a capricious notion. Dancing was in the Mosconi genes. Willie's cousins, Charlie and Louie, were part of a headline vaudeville team known as the Dancing Mosconis. Their father, also named Charlie, owned the South Philadelphia Dance Academy, and six-year-old Willie was enrolled as a pupil in the summer of 1919. But fate was a staunch ally. Uncle Charlie kept a pool table in the rear corner of the rehearsal hall, and Willie practiced his shots while waiting for his father to pick him up. The technique came naturally to him. In no time at all, he was running racks of balls. Uncle Charlie was the first to witness the youngster's instinctive feel for the game. It took a chance occurrence to make a believer of his father.

One day a friend of his father walked into the pool hall looking for a game but found the place empty.

"I'll play you, mister," Willie said.

The man smiled and broke the balls. Willie, climbing up and down from his box, ran the rack. The man summoned the elder Mosconi, and under his father's watchful gaze, Willie ran a second rack, then a third. Joseph Mosconi had seen enough pool to recognize the difference between skill and wizardry. He was, at bottom, a practical man, and he knew better than to resist the inevitable. Willie's career was underway, with his father acting as guide.

Billed as the Child Prodigy, Willie was sent forth on a round of

An exhibition star at the age of seven, Willie Mosconi is shown with Ralph Greenleaf, then world's champion. Willie's appearance poster carried this accurate prediction by Greenleaf: "Having defeated the seven-year-old Willie Mosconi 50 to 46 I have no hesitancy in saying he will be the future world's champion." Wide World Photo

exhibition matches in neighborhood pool halls at twenty-five dollars a game. At the age of seven, he was already something of a phenomenon, and one wily promoter had the inspiration to book him in a game against Ralph Greenleaf, then in his second year as world champion. Greenleaf, of course, won the match, but Willie put on a crowd-pleasing show, and promoters started referring to him as the Juvenile Champion. It was a title he was soon called upon to defend against a ten-year-old female prodigy by the name of Ruth McGinnis. Willie disposed of her easily, running forty balls in his first turn at the table.

Now, with no new worlds to conquer and growing weary of the grind, the young champion racked his cue stick and retired from competition.

"I was disenchanted and confused," Willie recalled some years later. "First my father tried to stop me from playing, then he went overboard in the other direction. I just didn't feel like playing any more."

Ten years would pass before he picked up a cue stick again, and once more it was chance that intervened. In 1930, with the country sinking into the depths of the Great Depression, Willie was pressed into leaving high school and going to work. Both his parents were ailing, and as the eldest of six children, Willie felt the weight of responsibility. He took a job as an upholsterer's apprentice at eight dollars a week. Within a year he had advanced to doing piece-work and was earning as much as forty dollars a week, not a poor wage in hard times, but that was as far as he got. He and his boss got into a scuffle when Willie was refused time off to watch the Philadelphia Athletics play the St. Louis Cardinals in the 1931 World Series. He saw the ball game, but he lost his job. On his way home, jobless and broke, Willie passed a local pool hall and noticed a sign in the window advertising a tournament with a first prize of seventy-five dollars.

"I used to play this game," Willie thought. "Maybe I still can."

He still could. He won the tournament easily, then entered a succession of similar competitions around the city, and won them all. Willie had found himself a new career.

During the next few years, he provided for his family by shooting pool for money in pool halls around the city and as far away as Camden, New Jersey. With his clean-cut, choir-boy looks, Willie gave the appearance of an easy mark. He found no shortage of seasoned opponents with plenty of cash and cues at the ready.

"That kind of competition was a trial by fire," Willie said. "It steeled me. I don't think a pool player can rise to the top and show championship mettle unless he sharked bets in his youth."

By 1933, now twenty years old, Willie was ready for a more demanding test. With the national championship tournament approaching, Izzie Goodman, owner of the Fox Billiard Academy, found himself without a contestant to sponsor. He had been backing Eddie Brown, one of Philadelphia's leading amateurs, but Brown fell ill and died suddenly a few weeks before the tournament was to start. Rather than forfeit his entry fee, Goodman chose young

Willie struck a determined pose for photographers during the 1933 world tournament in Chicago. Jimmy Caras, who was to win the title in 1936, watched with arms folded. United Press International

Mosconi to carry the Fox colors. Willie responded by defeating the highly touted Andrew St. Jean to win the divisional competition, then won the sectional in New York City and moved on to the national tournament in Minneapolis. There, he finished second to George Kelly, qualifying for the world tournament in Chicago. He came within one shot of winning it. Willie lost his match to Erwin Rudolph, the eventual champion, by one ball and finished in a four-way tie for second place.

His performance attracted the attention of the Brunswick-Balke-Collender Company, the pioneer manufacturer of billiard equipment, which signed him to an exhibition contract. Almost immediately, Brunswick sent him on a grueling 112-day, cross-country tour with the legendary Ralph Greenleaf, who had held the world title in all but three years since 1919. Willie managed to win fifty of their 107 matches, but more significantly, Greenleaf provided the younger player with an invaluable education.

"I watched him like a hawk," Willie remembered. "I learned all his little tricks, and I studied the way he played position. He sometimes ran whole racks without having to make a long shot."

It was during the Greenleaf tour that Willie caught the eye of Sylvester Livingston, a well-known booking agent and the most famous pool-hall impresario of his time. Livingston added Willie to his stable of billiard players and booked him on a circuit of exhibitions from New York to Florida to Chicago and back to New York. It was a tough grind. From early fall through the spring, Willie was on the road. He sometimes played three or four exhibitions a day in as many small towns. He ate on the run, slept in flop-house hotels, played on warped tables in dingy rooms, and earned barely enough to keep himself going. But he learned a lot from Livingston. It was Livingston who taught him that you cannot let up when playing big-time pool.

"Willie," he once told his young protégé, "if there is one thought I want to leave with you when I am no longer here, it is this: When you have the knife in, twist it."

"That is the best advice anyone ever gave me," Willie said.

It would be quite a while, however, before Willie turned his lessons to profit. During the next five years, he often performed well but was unable to break through in championship play. When Greenleaf faltered, players like Jimmy Caras and Andrew Ponzi were there to scoop up the stake. Willie's star seemed to be fading.

In the spring of 1940, he was not invited to compete in a six-man tournament to determine the world title. Later that year, it appeared he would be passed over again as billiard-hall owners chose players to represent their rooms in what would be the longest world-championship tournament ever held. It was to be played in six cities over a span of twenty-four weeks, from November 1940 to May 1941. The field would be expanded to eight contestants, with each playing 224 games—thirty-two against each of his seven opponents. As late as October, Willie had received no invitations. But a few weeks before competition was to start, Bob McGirr, owner of McGirr's Billiard Academy on Broadway, offered to sponsor Willie's return to tournament play. As it turned out, McGirr had carved himself a small slice of billiard history.

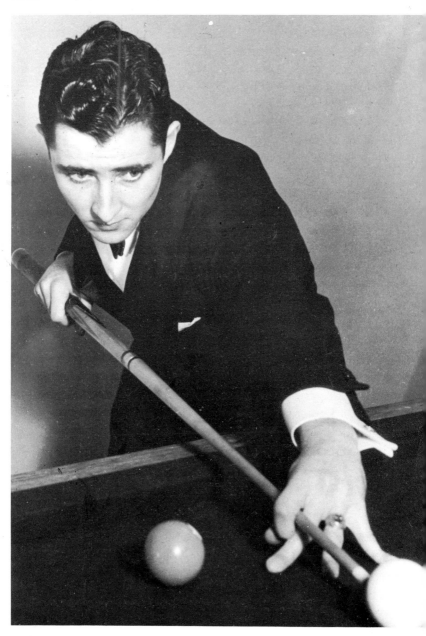

At the age of twenty-eight, Willie won the world's title in 1941.
Wide World Photo

Willie played as if the genie had just been sprung from the bottle. He did not merely win the tournament, he demolished the field, shattering records as he went. He finished with a mark of 176–48, thirty-three games ahead of second-place Ponzi. In the process, he ran a hundred or more balls fifty times and shut out nine opponents 125–0, five times right from the break. It was, by all measure, an astounding performance, and Willie, quite suddenly, was propelled onto the center of a stage reserved for only a handful of sports figures.

He had all the ingredients to fill the role. He combined a mechanical efficiency with the style and flair of a showman. He was both volatile and serene, street-tough yet gracious. When he stepped to the table he moved briskly, with an athlete's grace, the heels of his highly polished shoes tapping out a staccato beat on the wooden platform. Then, as he prepared to shoot, his engaging, movie-star features would take on a hard-eyed intensity as he sighted down the shaft of his cue stick like a sniper drawing a bead on his target. He made his shots in sustained bursts, gathering speed as he went. An opponent once complained that he felt punchy, sitting in his chair and watching as Mosconi ran rack after rack.

With his first championship under his belt, Willie put a virtual stranglehold on the world title. He held it for fifteen of seventeen years, surrendering it only in 1943 to Ponzi and in 1949 to Caras. Along the way, he inscribed his name alongside every record in the books. On March 19, 1954, in an exhibition in Springfield, Ohio, he ran 526 consecutive balls, the equivalent of thirty-five racks, breaking his own record while setting a new one that has never been approached. The run took two hours and ten minutes, during which time Willie averaged four balls a minute.

Two years later, in Kinston, North Carolina, the forty-three-year-old Mosconi staged what many considered the greatest display of pool shooting in history. He disposed of the seven leading challengers to his title in straight sets, winning all fourteen games. In his final match, he ran 150-and-out in the first inning against "Cowboy" Jimmy Moore. His sovereignty was now total; he had eliminated all legitimate challengers. World tournaments were suspended for

This was a frequent scene in the 1940's and 1950's, with two Willies, Mosconi and Hoppe, sharing the billiard-championship spotlight. Shown here after the 1951 world's competition, Mosconi had achieved his tenth pocket-billiards title and Hoppe had won his eleventh three-cushion crown.

seven years, and Willie, in effect, retired as champion.

He was not exactly idle in retirement. Although the end of formal competition took some of the shine from the game, Willie remained a national attraction. He continued to travel the country, giving as many as three hundred exhibitions a year. He acted as technical adviser for the 1961 movie *The Hustler,* tutoring the film's star, Paul Newman, setting up and often making the more difficult shots as the camera flashed from Newman's eyes to Willie's hands. In the seventies, he became something of a television celebrity and a hero to a new generation when he played and invariably defeated the real-life

Paul Newman, star of the motion picture *The Hustler*, got expert advice from Willie, who served as technical adviser on the film and executed many of the shots attributed to Newman and co-star Jackie Gleason.

pool hustler Minnesota Fats in a succession of TV extravaganzas. He competed regularly in pro-am golf tournaments, shooting in the mid- to upper-seventies and, more than once, carried home a trophy for his efforts.

But as he approached his seventieth birthday in 1983, Willie began winding down. He worked for a while as a goodwill ambassador at several Atlantic City hotel/casinos and still gave an occasional exhibition. But the years on the road had taken their toll, and he welcomed the opportunity to relax with his wife, Flora, in their Haddon Heights, New Jersey home. The pool table in the basement, the only one he had ever owned, was now used mainly as a place for Flora to store the laundry when she removed it from the dryer. Rarely was its clear plastic cover peeled back and the custom-made cue stick removed from its case.

Retired now from tournament competition, Willie is busy with a heavy schedule of exhibition appearances.

In 1991, I began working with Willie on his autobiography, *Willie's Game,* which was published two years later. For the better part of six months, we held weekly interview sessions in the Mosconi kitchen, lunching on pepperoni pizzas and delving into Willie's past. After one such session, we went down to the basement to select from a vast store of photographs those that might be suitable for publication. Then Willie, his gray eyes twinkling, steered me in the direction of the table.

"Wanna see me run a rack?" he asked.

He set the balls in a perfect triangle and flicked the nose ball from the front of the pack. He spotted the cue quickly and drilled the loose ball into the corner pocket. The cue ball veered right and sprayed open the pack except for a solid cluster at the center. Willie ran five balls in a matter of seconds, then surveyed the table.

"Looks like I didn't leave myself much," he said. But his playful smile betrayed him. "You think the fourteen might go?" There was no time to answer. He stroked smoothly. The fourteen ball scudded into the right-corner pocket. The other eight balls scattered like shards across the table.

"Now," he said, "I can see every shot in sequence. I know which ball will be left at the end of the rack and within two inches of where it will be." With his cue stick he pointed to the nine ball, then to a spot about six inches from the far left-corner pocket.

From that point on, everything happened quickly. "Three ball in the side pocket, twelve in the corner." He was on his way to the next spot before the ball dropped in the pocket. Every shot was an easy one. The cue ball behaved with the precision of a marionette drawn by its strings. Willie was playing from memory, performing a choreography that he had rehearsed for nearly seven decades. Finally, he nudged the six ball into the far-corner pocket. The cue kissed the rail and rolled to the center of the table. The last remaining ball had a yellow stripe; the nine ball. It was lying about five inches from the corner pocket, on the left side of the table.

"Nothin' to this game," Willie said.

Willie Mosconi's
WINNING POCKET BILLIARDS

1
Tools of the Trade

Introduction to the Table and Equipment

As in most other sports, equipment for the playing of pocket billiards has undergone refinements through the years. For the most part, however, equipment specifications and game rules have remained standard since the mid-1800's. I feel that an outline of these modern specifications may be helpful to you.

Table Specifications: All versions of pocket billiards are played on a rectangular table twice as long as it is wide, with $4^1/_2$ by 9 feet generally accepted as official tournament size. Finely woven wool cloth is stretched over the rubber cushions and table bed. When this cloth is cleaned, it should be brushed from the head to the foot of the table to keep the nap smooth. The foot end of the table is where the balls are racked.

End rails of the table are marked with three equally spaced diamonds or dots, and side rails are equipped with six such dots to designate playing boundaries and guide the player in computing bank-shot angles. You will learn to use table-rail markers as points of reference as you tackle the fascinating geometry of pocket billiards.

Study the accompanying illustration to familiarize yourself with table markings. Head and foot strings are not drawn on the table, but are only imaginary lines joining specific side-rail dots. Most pocket-billiards games start with a break shot from behind the head string; this string is also the boundary behind which you must shoot with "cue ball in hand" after a cue-ball scratch or fault. A foot spot is affixed to the table as the center of the imaginary foot string. Balls are racked on this spot to start a game, and during the course of play individual balls that have been pocketed illegally or shot off the

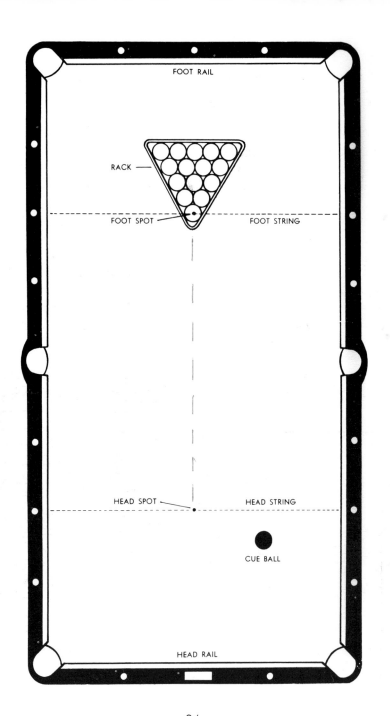

FOOT RAIL

RACK

FOOT SPOT

FOOT STRING

HEAD SPOT

HEAD STRING

CUE BALL

HEAD RAIL

24

table must be returned to the spot or as close behind it as possible if the spot is covered by another ball.

Openings of the two side pockets are about $5\frac{1}{2}$ inches wide, while pocket openings of the four corner pockets are 5 inches wide. Since corner pockets usually afford easier shot angles, their openings are smaller in compensation. The point of difference in side- and corner-pocket openings is to equalize the difficulty in shotmaking.

Racking the Balls: Regulation size is $2\frac{1}{4}$-inch diameter for all object balls and cue ball. Object balls are numbered 1 through 15, and each ball is of a different solid color or is banded for quick identification. In a later chapter on game rules you will be instructed on how to position balls in the rack by number to start various games.

In racking the balls, it is important that they be kept in a tight cluster by pressing them forward within the triangle with the thumbs (center), then carefully removing the triangle to keep contact between all balls.

Cues are usually stamped by weight in ounces. Most players use a 20- or 21-ounce cue, generally about 57 inches long.

In racking balls, it is important that they be moved to proper position at the foot spot and held in tight formation while the rack is lifted. A "loose" rack, one in which balls are separated, however slightly, will not break properly. Photographs in this section will show you how to rack balls expertly.

Cues, Mechanical Bridge: Like baseball bats and golf clubs, pocket-billiard cues are available in a variety of weights to suit an individual player's requirements. The average length is 57 inches, and weights vary from 16 to 22 ounces. I use a 57-inch, $19^1/_2$-ounce cue with a $12^1/_2$-millimeter tip. As a beginner, you will be well

Use the mechanical bridge as a cue support for long shots.

advised to select a medium-weight cue; later, you may experiment with variations when you are able to detect differences in cue action. Many modern billiard centers provide trained instructors to assist players in cue selection. Take advantage of this help.

The length of a billiard cue is a factor in enabling you to reach difficult shots, but situations will arise in a game when neither the cue nor your arms are long enough to make the desired shot. When this happens, use the mechanical bridge without hesitation. I have seen too many players, myself included, occasionally miss a critical shot by stretching into an awkward body position instead of employing the mechanical bridge. Learn to use it; then don't neglect it when it is needed.

Let's move now into succeeding chapters on fundamentals of shotmaking, a section of this book I urge you to read thoroughly and to review frequently as your ability sharpens. There never was a sports champion who dared neglect concentration on the fundamentals of his game. Study, practice, and build on fundamentals for steady improvement in your game of pocket billiards.

2
Take Your Cue

Cue Selection, Grip, and Stance

This is the first of several preliminary chapters in which I discuss the fundamentals of pocket-billiard play. Forgive the repetition, but I feel compelled to reemphasize the importance of this section to beginner and advanced player alike. I have observed too many otherwise promising students of the game stall and even backslide from a level of ability because of their neglect of fundamentals. A bad habit, formed and not corrected early in a player's development, is likely to hinder his progress forever. Application of proper techniques in the following basic elements will enable you to progress to the maximum of your ability:

1. Cue selection, grip, and stance
2. Basic bridge and variations
3. Stroke and follow-through
4. Hitting the cue ball
5. Basic shotmaking

In this and other sections of the book, I make frequent comparisons between golf, particularly putting, and pocket billiards. I enjoy both sports, and the techniques of play are similar, at least for purposes of illustration. The comparison of billiards to golf breaks down in a hurry on the fairway, but on the putting green the stance, grip, and stroke very nearly duplicate the approach needed on a table with six holes.

The best of putters and billiard players often develop peculiarities in their style. Don't copy these unique characteristics unless you find them most helpful after a long period of trial and error and qualified instruction. Master the accepted fundamentals, and practice. You will be a winner.

Cue Selection: As a beginner, select a cue of average length and

29

Find the balance point of a cue by sliding it along your finger until the weight of the butt end equals that of the shaft.

weight; let's say 57 inches and 19 or 20 ounces. Later, as you practice, experiment to determine the weight best suited to you. If you find this game as challenging and fascinating as I'm sure you will, your next step may be the purchase of a personal cue or rental at your billiard center of one custom-fitted to you.

Pocket-billiard cues are nearly six feet long to permit your reaching the maximum number of shots in a comfortable position. Balance is important, too. A good cue is one whose weight distribution permits the player to position his right-hand grip and left-hand bridge properly and without arm strain. This and other references to hand and arm are designed to instruct the right-handed player. You left-handed players, of whom there are a growing number, will reverse such designations.

If you purchase your own cue, use sandpaper to taper the cue tip into a half-moon shape. The cue tip should be rounded, not flat.

Grip Lightly: The "where" and "how" of your right-hand grip at the butt end of the cue are of equal importance. Where you grip the cue determines your ability to stroke freely and smoothly. How you grip the cue is a vital factor in the delicate touch and full follow-through so important to successful shotmaking.

First, let us determine where to grip the cue. Start by finding its balance point. Slide the cue across your finger until it balances, with the butt-end weight equaling that of the shaft. Engineers call this the fulcrum point, and youngsters recognize it as the exact middle of a teeter-totter. Now slide your hand three to six inches behind this

1 – 2 hand widths

Position the grip; then slide your right hand back three to five inches from the balance point.

point to position the grip. Too great a variance from this recommended grip position will either cramp your stoke or extend your stance awkwardly. Both faults are common, but certainly avoidable. Start with the proper grip, then check its position from time to time as you play or practice.

Now for the "how" of a proper grip—and I use that word only because it is in common usage. The word "grip" frequently denotes a firm handshake or tight grasp of an object. Forget both definitions when you approach the grip of a billiard cue. The grip I speak of here is more closely related to that on a teacup handle—delicate, and involving only the thumb and first three fingers.

Illustrations here of the proper cue grip tell the story better than I can with words. I shall elaborate only to spell out the importance of this fundamental. A light and relaxed grip with the thumb and three

The key to a smooth stroke is a light grip on the cue with the thumb and first three fingers.

fingers is the key to smooth and proper cue force in stroking the ball. Stranglehold grips probably are the prime offenders in forcing players into excessive stroke force, one of the most common playing faults. You can produce all the cue force ever needed in this game with a relaxed finger grip and the pendulum action of your right arm.

Let's return to the golf putting green for a comparison. In putting, the left hand guides back the club, and the right hand—gripping the putter with thumb and fingers—moves the club into the stroke. On the billiard table, the left-hand bridge guides the cue, which is moved straight through the stroke with a minimum of right-arm and wrist power.

Mark this down as another frequent checkpoint. As you approach a shot, relax your grip, and then regrip with concentration on thumb and three-finger contact with the cue. Then, to relax further, "waggle" the cue into the stroke as you would in preparation for a golf swing.

Comfortable Stance: I've seen all kinds of stances, and I can safely say there are as many unorthodox stances by billiard players as by subway straphangers. Not all unusual stances are necessarily bad, but many are, and the only way to avoid the risk of an unbalanced stance is to learn the correct position for body and feet—then stick with it.

Here are two points of reference. A good billiard stance puts the player into a balanced and comfortable position, and centers his head over the cue in the line of aim.

How do you achieve a good stance? Eventually, you won't be following this ritual before every shot, but for now, begin by standing erect, facing the direction of your shot. The position of the cue ball will determine how far back from the table you stand. For this exercise in proper form, however, stand about one foot back from the table, with your weight evenly distributed on both feet.

Now, turn both feet slightly to the right and bend forward at the waist. Your feet should be six to eight inches apart and your weight still equally distributed. This accepted billiard stance permits your right arm to swing freely and your left arm to be extended as

To assume a balanced and comfortable stance, begin by facing your shot squarely (top photo), with your weight equally distributed on both feet. Then turn your hips slightly to the right as shown in the lower photo.

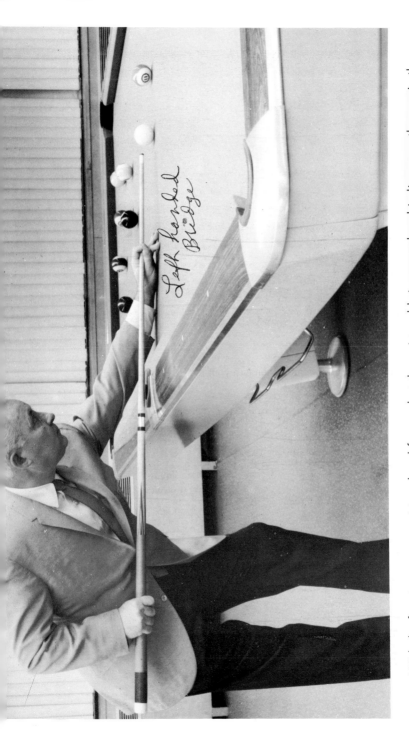

Left handed Bridge

6" ~ 8"

With the feet in proper position, bend forward at the waist and bring your head in line over the cue in the completed stance. Your feet should be no more than six inches apart.

This front view illustrates how the proper stance will bring the player's head automatically in line with the cue.

Your body will be close to, or against, the table for shots like this one across the width of the table.

With the cue ball close to the rail, you must take up a stance farther back. The position of the feet and body remains the same.

straight as possible into the left-hand bridge. Your left knee will be bent a bit more than your right, and your body will be free to move slightly forward with the stroke.

The distance of your body from the table must vary according to cue-ball position. A shot with the cue ball at or near the cushion will require assuming a stance farther back. As you stretch for a shot in the middle of the table, of course, your body will be closer to, or against, the table.

Whatever the shot situation, maintain the elements of this basic stance. The keys here are balance, freedom of stroke movement, and position of the head above the cue.

We've come to the bridge; now let's cross it.

3
Construction Ahead

Basic, Rail, and V-Bridges

A roadway bridge is defined as a firm support structure, and there's no reason to change that definition for a billiard-cue bridge. The purpose of a billiard bridge is to form your hand into as firm and steady a support as possible for the cue, which will travel between your finger structure in stroking the ball. Let's proceed with some basic bridge building.

Basic Bridge: Because the standard bridge is the one you will be using for 90 percent of your shots, it deserves most of your attention and practice. It's as easy as clenching your fist.

In fact, start by making a fist with your left hand. Extend your left arm and place your fist on the table, palm down. Open your thumb and forefinger and lay the cue along your thumb between the knuckles. Draw your forefinger down over the top of the cue and use your thumb to press that fingertip against the middle knuckle of your second finger. You now have a channel through which the cue can slide, but that's not enough. A billiard bridge needs a base of support broader than a fist.

With the heel of your hand resting on the table, separate and extend the last three fingers into as wide an area of support as possible without strain. You now have four distinct and solid contacts with the table and have "built" a sound bridge of finger-girders and a palm-heel pedestal.

If your hand is arched properly, the fleshy part of your thumb will no longer be touching the table, and if your fingers are well spread, the cue shaft will be above the middle of your third finger. Illustrations here from various angles will enable you to compare the bridge you have formed with the one I use. Observe the snug fit of the cue in the channel formed by my thumb and forefinger.

39

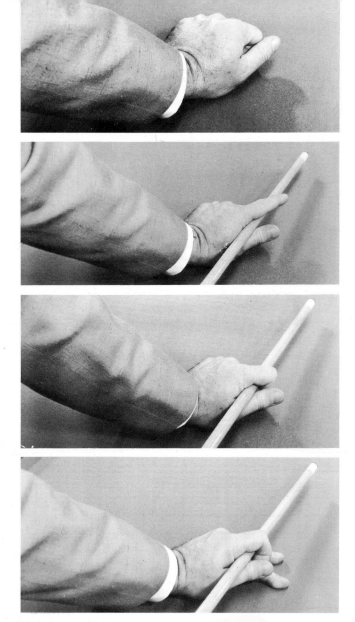

To form a basic bridge (top to bottom), make a fist and place it on the table palm down. Open your thumb and forefinger and lay the cue along your thumb. Draw your forefinger down over the top of the cue, then separate and extend the last three fingers into a broad base of support. Note that the hand turns slightly inward at the wrist to complete the bridge.

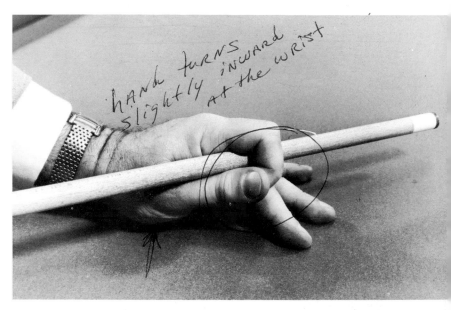

hand turns inward slightly at the wrist

The cue fits snugly in the channel formed by the thumb and forefinger in these right- and left-side photographs of the basic bridge. Fingers are widespread but not strained.

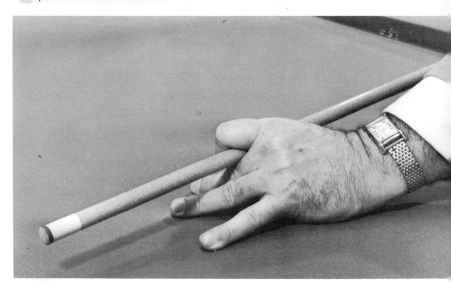

"Snug" in this sense means that the flesh of your thumb and finger moves as you move the cue back and forth in stroking.

Too loose a finger channel is a common bridge fault, as is the tendency of some players to pull their forefinger away from the knuckle of their second finger. Since the bridge is so important a foundation of billiard play, frequently check your hand structure against the photographs in this chapter to make sure you are not straying from proper form.

Before we move into variations, it is well to repeat that the basic bridge is the one that is used most often and that should be used in all possible situations because it is the most dependable. It can be employed with as little as ten inches between the rail and the cue ball.

Once you master the standard bridge structure, you will be ready for later advice on altering it slightly to elevate or lower the cue for special shots.

A basic bridge should be used whenever possible, even when the cue ball is as close to the rail as shown here.

Rail Bridge: Part of the exciting challenge of billiards is the fact that the player is confronted with shots at all table positions. This often means that the cue ball or object ball may be situated against or too near the table rail to permit use of the basic bridge. I have two solutions to enable you to make these shots.

1. Assume that the cue ball is two to six inches from the rail—too little table space to form a basic bridge. Tuck your thumb under your forefinger and rest your outstretched fingers and palm on the rail. Separate your forefinger and insert the cue through this channel alongside your thumb. The two fingers and thumb provide points of pressure to guide the cue.

2. The second rail-bridge situation arises when the cue ball is frozen to the cushion and you face other than a straightaway shot. Use the rail-bridge cue channel between your first two fingers, but rest only your forefinger on the cushion while your other three fingers extend to the table for support.

When the cue ball is so close to the rail that it prevents you from using a basic bridge, employ this rail bridge by tucking back your thumb and sliding the cue between your first two fingers.

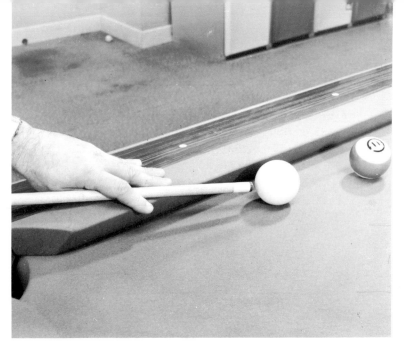

Two other variations of rail bridges show how the forefinger can extend over the rail (top photograph), or how two fingers may rest on the table (lower photograph) for firmer support.

Remember on all rail shots not to elevate the cue more than is necessary.

V-Bridge: During the course of play, you will be faced with shots in which the cue ball is positioned in front of one or more object balls—too close to hit without elevating the cue markedly. The only solution: elevate the cue.

In these shot situations the V-Bridge is necessary to elevate the cue over obstructing balls. Use thumb pressure to keep the cue firm in the V-channel.

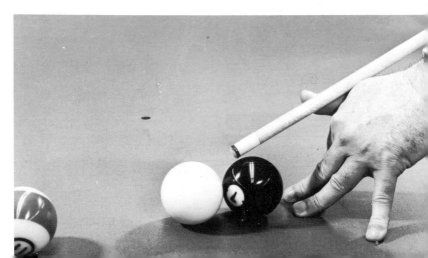

Use the mechanical bridge to reach long shots. The handle should be held against the table, and the stroke should be made by gripping the cue at the end with your thumb and first two fingers. To elevate the cue (photograph at right), turn the mechanical bridge on end.

Without touching any balls (a foul) position your hand behind the intervening ball and arch your wrist by extending all four fingers to the table. In doing so, you no longer have the use of the finger-and-thumb cue channel of a basic bridge. Do the next best thing and form a vee by turning your thumb upward and using it to hold the cue against the top of your hand along the knuckle of the first finger. The cue will slide along this vee and over the obstructing ball as you elevate the butt end of the cue.

Experiment by varying the placement of your support fingers until you determine the arrangement of firmest cue support under these admittedly awkward circumstances.

Mechanical Bridge: I introduce you now to the device mentioned in our chapter on playing equipment. Its simple purpose is to provide cue support for shots too far to reach with your arms. Using it prevents you from committing a foul by not having one foot on the floor as you shoot and from overextending your arms and body into an unsteady shooting position.

Move the mechanical bridge into position carefully, remembering that disturbing balls is also a foul, and hold the handle end firmly against the table with your left hand. Bridge your cue in the appropriate slot, and stroke with a three-finger grip on the butt end. The stroke must be smooth to keep your cue from jumping out of the slot.

Also illustrated here is the use of the mechanical bridge to shoot over intervening balls. You would be using the hand V-Bridge if this shot were close enough. Since it isn't, turn the mechanical bridge on its side to elevate the cue.

Before you chalk up and stroke, remember that all billiard body positions—stance, grip, and bridge—are designed to keep your head over the cue in line of aim.

The pool cue must go straight.

47

Ventura Beach, Calif

Good took R.V. Resort

one of Adam's rib

x Made a

Coast

Speaker - Miracle

Stanley 70 in 2011

July 25, 1941 / 70

giveback · org
email
+ password
sets up
your own
website

DOPPA Dec 27, 1945

4
A Delicate Touch

Stroke Soft with Follow-through

Remember my comparison of billiards to golf putting? Picture this. An enthusiastic golfer equips himself with the finest of clubs, spends hours at the driving range learning to power the ball 250 yards, dresses in flashy togs, and then never breaks 90 because he three-putts nearly every green. He could better spend his practice time and money learning to stroke rather than jab his putts.

Back to our billiard table, we may find the same enthusiast who has a "picture" stance, grip, and bridge and who has developed a superior sense of aiming, yet seldom is a winner. I'll bet my ivory-inlaid cue his fault lies in his stroke control, speed, and follow-through.

Proper stance, grip, and bridge are vital preparations to effective stroking, but it's your movement of the cue that propels the ball and determines where it rolls dead. I'll devote more space later to a discussion of "position play." For now, as you approach stroke control, bear in mind the necessity of predetermining cue-ball action after it strikes the object-ball target.

Chalk Up Before Every Shot: There you are, already in your stance, and now I'm asking you to stand up and perform a quick but vital preliminary.

Apply chalk lightly to the cue tip, now and before every stroke, to avoid miscues—the "dub shots" of billiards.

Cue tips are made of leather or composition material whose texture does not provide friction sufficient to assure firm contact with the polished cue ball. And because the tip will come in contact with the curved surface of a ball, it needs the increased friction of chalk to avoid slipping off the intended point of contact.

This fact becomes even more important as you progress into

Turn the chalk, never the cue, in a light back-and-forth motion or half-turn to deposit a light film of chalk on the cue tip before each shot.

shotmaking that calls for stroking the ball at points off dead center.

Here's the proper way of applying chalk to the cue tip. Don't turn the cue, turn the chalk in application. One light back-and-forth motion or half-turn, forward and back, is enough to deposit a light film of chalk on the tip. Chalk should never be applied so that it builds up a layer or flakes. Excessive chalk on the tip defeats its purpose.

Use a Short Stroke: Now return to your stance, facing the shot with your feet turned slightly to the right. Your grip with three fingers and thumb is three to six inches behind the cue's balance point, and you have formed a steady finger bridge to guide the shaft.

About eight inches of cue shaft should extend from your bridge channel to the cue ball. Short stroking action provides better control, and in this position your backstroke will be no longer than four to six inches.

The spring action of your arm and wrist will provide the amount of power needed to send the cue ball anywhere on the table. A longer stroke only increases the chance of off-target contact of cue tip and cue ball.

Warm-up Stroking: Golfers "waggle" a club before hitting, and baseball players take practice swings as they await a pitch. They do it to relax and loosen up in preparation for positive action. In our

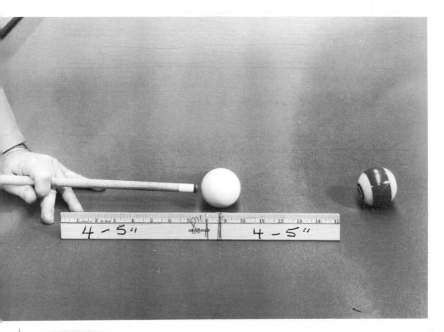

4 - 5"   4 - 5"

No more than eight inches of cue shaft should extend from your bridge to the cue ball as you prepare to shoot.

BACK stroke
4 - 6"

Two or three smooth practice strokes of the cue will keep your arm and wrist loose before you stroke the ball.

sport of billiards, we use warm-up stroking for the same purpose.

The use of three or four rhythmic warm-up strokes before stroking the cue ball will serve to loosen your arm and wrist, and center your concentration upon the shot at hand.

At this point you have selected the object ball and surveyed the table to determine position for the next shot. In addition to helping you relax, the warm-up movements will aid you in "grooving" the stroke toward the intended point of contact with the ball.

Just don't get reckless in your preliminary stroking. Any accidental contact of cue and ball is a foul.

Stroke and Speed: If there was a sure-fire formula for perfect stroke control and speed, every billiard player would be an unbeatable champion and our sport would face extinction for lack of challenge.

The fact is, all billiard shots present challenges, and in infinite variety. You must plan and aim every stroke to pocket an intended object ball (with some strategy exceptions) and to send the cue ball into the best possible position for the next shot.

Don't shy from words like acquired "feel" and "sense" of stroking. They are the most expressive I can think of to describe the necessary ingredients to improve ability. The "feel" a good player develops for each stroke situation is the result of practice and concentration, and is only slightly related to natural talent.

The key words in billiard shotmaking are "soft" and "softer." Properly installed billiard tables are as level and true as man can make them. The balls are perfectly round, and this combination means that little force is needed to set the balls in motion and keep them rolling to desired positions.

Illustrate this to yourself by noting how little force is required to stroke the ball from near the head rail to the foot rail and back, as you will in "lagging" to determine the first shooter to start a game; or how a "soft" stroke can send the ball around the table, striking all four cushions.

These are only tests of speed. A later chapter on practice techniques will concentrate on gauging speed of stroke to help you develop the "feel" required to improve your ability.

Though it may sound a little like a dance step, here's the tempo of a billiard stroke—short, level, smooth, and soft.

Stroke "Through" the Ball: Good golfers and baseball players who make use of practice swings also know the value of the follow-through—that smooth flow of action after the ball is hit. Neither I nor anyone else can tell you that the action you take after you hit the ball will affect its line of travel. After impact, there's nothing you can do to change your shot.

But it is as true in billiards as in any other sport that the follow-through is pertinent to the entire action, and is very important in smoothing out the stroke motion and putting a finishing touch to the shot.

Your determination to follow through is a guarantee against jabbing or poking the ball, which are results of jerking the stroke up short. In billiards, a "jerk" is defined either as an impolite player or as an incomplete—and very likely unsuccessful—stroke.

Stroke short, level, smooth, soft, and "through" the ball. A proper follow-through will send your cue straight through the area occu-

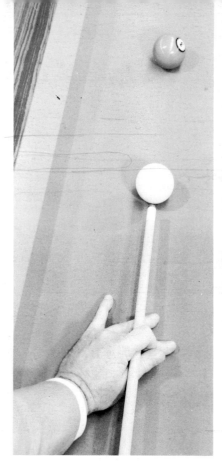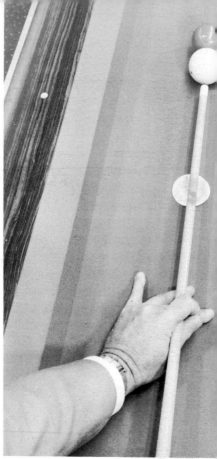

Follow-through is important in a billiard stroke. Note how the cue is sent through the area occupied by the cue ball before it was hit.

pied by the cue ball before it was hit. As you stroke through the ball, your right elbow will drop slightly and your grip hand should pivot backward at the wrist to keep the cue traveling on a level plane.

If you started a backstroke with eight inches of cue shaft from finger bridge to cue ball, there should be twelve inches extended after follow-through. Infrequent exceptions will be necessary when shooting with an elevated cue or into a close ball cluster.

Start now to make full follow-through a part of each stroke. If you must, exaggerate it to form the habit. With practice, your follow-through will become as natural as forming a bridge.

Right handed Bridge

This photo sequence, from top to bottom, illustrates complete stroke action from aim to follow-through. Observe that my head is steady and that the cue remains level.

5
Get on the Ball

Stop, Follow, and Draw Shots

The "moment of truth" in billiards is that split-second when cue tip meets cue ball and sets in motion the shot you have planned. All your preparation—grip, stance, bridge, and aim—is focused at moving the cue ball in a precise path required to hit and send the object ball into a pocket.

With the cue ball in motion, all you can do is watch—and hope. Assuming you have learned earlier lessons well, your chances for a successful shot are good. The *ker-thunk* of a pocketed object ball is a gratifying sound.

But I have indicated in previous chapters that playing to win requires execution of a series of successful shots. The object of most games of pocket billiards is to pocket in succession as many balls as possible before you relinquish the table to your opponent after a miss, foul, or in defensive strategy.

This calls for playing position—stroking the cue ball so that it not only drives the desired object ball into a pocket but also rolls into the best possible position for the next shot. Control of the cue ball can make you a winner.

Center-Ball Stroking: The vast majority of shots can, and should, be executed by stroking the cue ball at its exact center. At this point of cue-ball contact, you have the surest control of its line of roll to the object ball.

To strike the cue ball at dead center, use a standard bridge with normal finger elevation to bring the cue tip in line with the ball's center spot. With the cue level, stroke smoothly with a full follow-through.

Properly stroked, the center-ball shot will stop the cue ball after its impact with an object ball. This will be true only when the shot

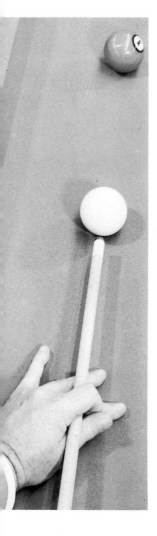

These overhead and rear views illustrate a center-ball stroke. A standard bridge is used to produce dead-center cue impact.

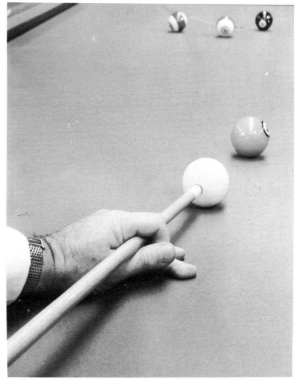

calls for reasonably full impact with the object ball. When you "cut" the object ball—hit it to angle sharply—the cue ball may also angle away, even in a center-ball shot.

Nevertheless, the stop shot will be a valuable technique in many situations in which you want the cue ball to remain in the same relative position from which you moved the object ball.

Here is a side view of cue position for a center-ball shot.

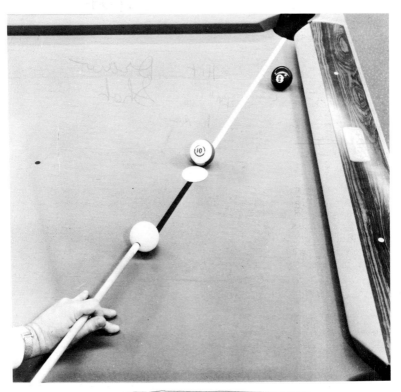

As diagrammed here, a center-ball stroke produces a stop shot, which keeps the cue ball near the position occupied by the object ball before impact.

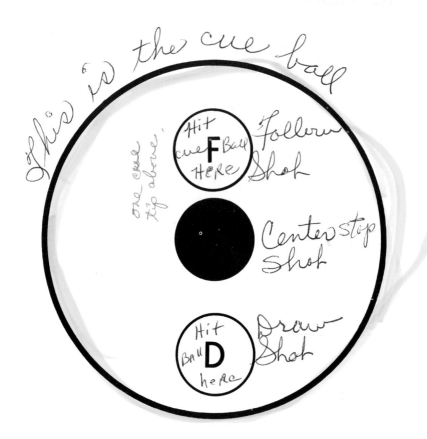

This is the cue ball

one cue tip above.

Hit cue Ball HERE **F** — Follow Shot

Center stop Shot

Hit Ball here **D** — Draw Shot

To produce a follow shot, strike the cue ball a cue-tip width above center. For a draw shot, the ball must be struck as far below center as possible, with the cue relatively level.

Follow Shot: Now comes our first variation in stroke to provide cue-ball control. It's called the follow shot simply because its execution sends the cue ball in the same general direction as the struck object ball.

Let's assume that you are shooting a ball into a corner pocket from a cue-ball position near the center of the table and that the next object ball in your sequence of strategy lies near the foot rail. A stop shot in this situation would leave the cue ball too far away and at a difficult angle from the next object ball.

A follow shot is the answer, and here's how to stroke it.

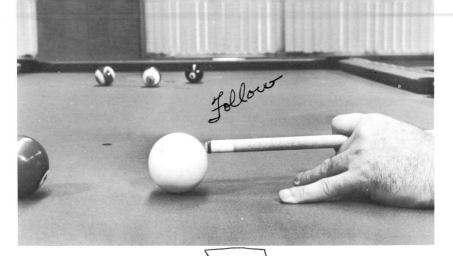

Follow

Bring the cue tip into position for a follow shot by elevating the bridge hand. Accomplish this by pulling your fingertips closer to your hand, forming a higher arch and cue channel.

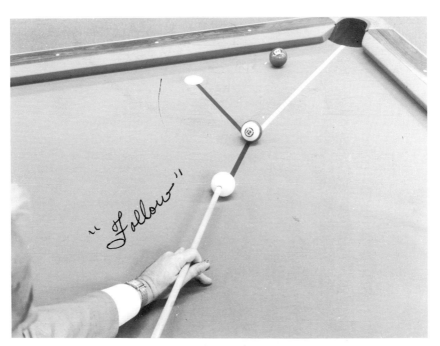

"Follow"

In a follow shot the cue ball moves forward after impact with the object ball. In this illustration the cue ball veers left because the object ball had to be angled to the right to be pocketed.

61

First of all, let me explain that the cue ball will "follow" only through the action of overspin. And to impart overspin to the cue ball, you must stroke it above center.

Remember what I've said about the value of keeping the cue level on all shots with very few exceptions? You can adhere to this rule and still stroke the follow shot. The solution is in your fingers.

Execute the follow shot by striking the cue ball a cue-tip width above center. Don't lower the butt of the cue to bring its tip into this position. This throws the cue off level and increases the danger of a miscue. To bring the cue tip into position for a follow stroke, elevate the bridge hand. Accomplish this by pulling your fingertips closer to your hand, forming a higher arch and cue channel. This bridge position elevates the cue tip to a follow-stroke impact level.

The follow-stroke bridge is illustrated from various angles in this chapter.

Take care to strike the ball only a cue-tip width above center, not higher, and follow through normally. And did you remember to chalk up before the shot? A properly chalked cue tip is vital to sure stroking of a follow shot.

Draw Shot. In practicing the follow shot, it doesn't take long to discover that this stroke is not the total solution to position play. In many situations the follow shot is plainly out of the question because it would send the cue ball away from the next object ball or,

By extending and spreading the fingers of your bridge hand, you will lower the cue tip into position for a draw shot.

Draw action on the cue ball pulls it back from impact with an object ball and into position for the next shot, as shown here.

worse, into the pocket for a "scratch." When you scratch—pocket the cue ball—any object ball pocketed in the same shot must be returned to the table, and your opponent takes over.

A stop shot should be your choice to avoid scratching in some situations. In others, in which you want the cue ball to roll backward from its object-ball impact, use the draw shot. "Draw" is the reverse of "follow," and means that you give the cue ball underspin to reverse its direction after impact with an object ball.

You're right. To apply draw to the cue ball, strike it below center—as low as possible with a level cue. The diagram in this chapter illustrates cue-ball impact points for center-ball, follow, and draw strokes. You will note that the draw shot calls for cue-tip impact at a point lower than a cue-tip width below center. A low impact point is required to give the ball decisive draw action.

You're right again. Lower the bridge—don't elevate the cue butt—to bring the cue tip into position for a draw shot. By extending and spreading the fingers of your bridge hand, you will lower the cue tip without altering the level of the cue.

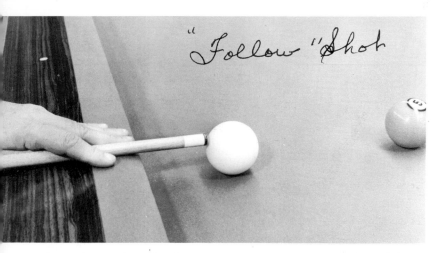

"Follow" Shot

From close to the rail, a follow shot (top photograph) or draw shot (lower photograph) can be executed with a normal rail bridge.

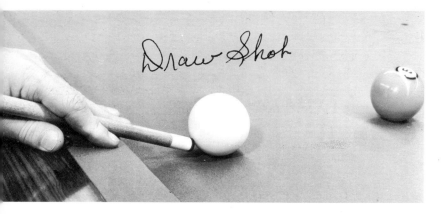

Draw Shot

As in the case with the follow shots, some draw-shot situations will require the use of other than a basic bridge. One such situation is pictured here to guide you. The butt end of the cue must be raised higher than normal to put the cue tip in draw-shot position with a rail or V-Bridge.

You can't spend practice time any better than in mastering center-ball, follow, and draw strokes. They form the stock-in-trade of a good billiard player—one who exercises maximum cue-ball control with a minimum of fancy maneuvers.

6
A Useful Twist

Application of English

Beginning pocket-billiard players would be well advised to skip concentration and practice on this lesson for the present. As a beginner, you can return to this section after your basic shotmaking sharpens a bit.

But since this book is intended to help beginners and advanced players alike, it is necessary at this point to include a brief chapter on "how" and "why" to apply English to the cue ball. Serious students of the game must develop a stroke for English and an awareness of its value in certain shot and position play situations.

Don't let English scare you. I stress the advanced nature of this stroke technique only because of its special applications. Centerball, draw, and follow shots generally will carry you around the table with successful shots and good cue-ball position. Resort to English only when you are confronted with the need to alter cue- or object-ball action radically.

What Is "English"? Don't ask me the origin of the word in this sense. I must defer to other specialists for an explanation of how "English" came to define unusual spin on a ball—billiard or otherwise. Some say it comes from "Angle," but I don't know. English is the application of abnormal spin on a ball that can alter its course before and after it strikes an object. Ball spin produces a curve on a baseball and hooking action on a bowling ball. Now let's close the "Mosconi School of Physics" and consider the practical application of English to the playing of billiards.

You've already learned that more than normal overspin on the cue ball—applied by stroking it above center—will produce a follow shot. And by stroking the ball below center, you can draw it back from object-ball impact with draw-shot underspin. English is

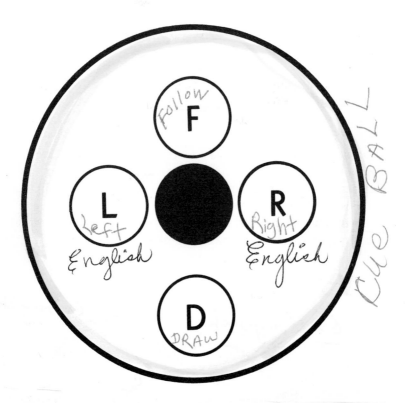

(handwritten annotations on figure: Follow, Left English, Right English, DRAW, Cue Ball)

Right or left English can be applied to the cue ball by striking it no more than a cue-tip width to the right or left of center.

an extension of these techniques, and produces either clockwise or counterclockwise spin on the cue ball, depending on where it is stroked.

Stroke for English: You can apply all the English ever required on the cue ball by stroking it no more than a cue-tip width to the right or left of center. As I pointed out on the follow shot, cue-tip impact farther than cue-tip width from center increases the likelihood of a miscue.

To stroke for English, use a standard bridge with the fingers of the bridge hand extended normally, as they are for a center-ball shot. The difference, of course, is that you will position the bridge hand to bring the cue top in line with a point of intended impact right or left of center.

With the cue tip chalked, take several warm-up strokes, then stroke firm and sharp with a full follow-through.

How English Affects the Cue Ball: Our description of English said that it affects ball action both before and after it strikes an object. This is the fact that makes proper control of English a bit complicated. In billiards, English alters the path of the cue ball to the object ball and changes cue-ball reaction after it strikes a cushion. English also affects the direction of a struck object ball, but I shall elaborate on that later.

By striking the cue ball to the right of center, you produce counterclockwise spin and therefore right English. Stroked right, the cue

Here's a player's eye view of cue position to produce right English.   Left English.

See page 77

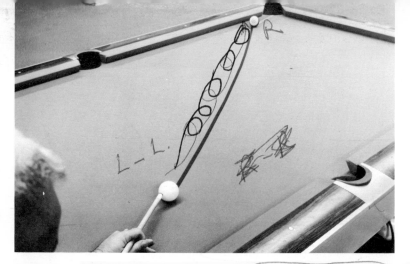

Application of English will cause the cue ball to curve in the direction of the English, left or right. The amount of curve increases with the length of the shot.

ball tends to curve right, with the amount of curve increasing with the length of the shot. You can see now why the application of English is a trifle tricky. In aiming a long shot with English, you must compensate for the curve of the cue ball as you aim its point of impact with the object ball.

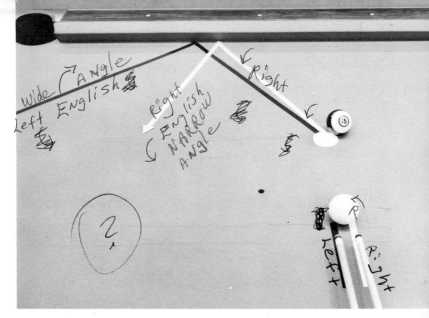

English affects the angle of cue-ball rebound after it strikes a cushion. The angle narrows as a result of right English, outlined here in white. The dark line illustrates the wider angle produced by left English. The effect would be reversed on banks to the cushion from the opposite angle.

Right English also adds speed to the cue ball, and widens its angle of deflection after it strikes a cushion, at least in straightforward shots to a cushion. In a difficult shot situation, these can be important factors in positioning the cue ball.

This cue-ball action—its path to an object ball, speed, and deflection angle off a cushion—is reversed when it is struck left of center. Left English sends the cue ball curving to the left, and again this principle applies: The longer the shot, the greater the curve. It also decreases the speed of the cue ball and narrows its angle after striking a cushion. The accompanying table diagram will, I hope, clear away any confusion resulting from this quick cadence of "rights" and "lefts."

This piece of advice bears repeating. English can be a useful, and on some occasions a necessary, stroke technique in your game strategy. It's well worth practicing, but only at a point in the development of your ability when you feel confident enough to move into this phase of advanced shotmaking.

7
In the Pocket

Hit the Object Ball and Score

Up to now, I've directed your attention to the necessary preliminaries to pocket-billiards play. Concentration on grip, stance, bridge, and stroke comprises the vital sequence of steps leading to movement and control of the cue ball.

Obviously, you can't play the game, much less win, by merely shoving the cue ball around the table. The cue ball must hit object balls within narrow limits of precision, sending them to designated pockets. What happens to the cue ball after it sends an object ball to a pocket is the key to setting up the next shot to start building what we call a "run," or series, of successful shots. High runs are the big thrills in billiards, and the ingredients of victory.

For now, however, let's concentrate on one object ball at a time.

It is time now to reopen the "Mosconi School of Applied Science." This lecture will be blessedly brief, and it never hurts any of us to think through the "why" of something. It's worth examining what happens when the cue ball strikes the object ball.

When the cue ball is stroked to give it either straightforward or reverse roll over its horizontal axis—follow, stop, or draw shot—it will move a struck-object ball at an angle equal to the angle of impact axis on the cue ball. (There's a mouthful for you.) While you're scratching your head, wondering why Mosconi doesn't switch to engineering, let me describe a simple experiment you can, and should, try.

Helpful Experiment: With chalk or a crayon, draw a line over the top and down the sides of an object ball in the direction of the intended pocket. Now draw a line on the cue ball that, if extended to the cushion, would be parallel to the line from object ball to pocket. Now place the cue ball in contact with the object ball, matching up

71

the lines on both. The point of impact necessary to pocket the ball is the point at which the lines touch.

Before the purists howl, I hasten to add that this simple experiment illustrated in this chapter does not take into account an allowable margin for impact error, and most certainly does not apply when English is applied to the cue ball.

For the moment, though, I hope this little exercise will help you grasp the principle of object-ball rejection. I've seen intense players study a shot, then apply chalk from their cue tip to the intended impact point on both cue ball and object ball. This sort of help in aiming would not be permitted in a match, but I see nothing wrong with it as a practice device. Just don't become dependent on it.

Which brings us to the main point of this chapter—to help you to develop an "eye" for sighting the object ball, aiming the cue ball, and to outline special strokes for certain advanced shotmaking.

Sighting: Who says the playing of pocket billiards does not involve exercise? Aside from bending in to a stance, which is good for most waistlines, there is considerable walking in our game. Some observers comment that I seem to circle the table more often than many other players during the course of a match. If I do, it's not only because I need the exercise. I also "stalk" the table to sight my shots.

It will not be necessary for you to walk around the table to line up each shot. Some will be relatively simple to plan and execute. Others, requiring a sharp angle of attack, should be surveyed from the direction of the intended pocket and from the point of impact. Such multiple sighting will serve to train your judgment in sizing up the shot at hand and others to follow.

As you survey a shot from several angles, I hope you remember our experiment. If you extend an imaginary line from the pocket through the object ball, it will emerge at the required point of impact. This position of contact remains the same regardless of cue-ball position.

Earlier, I mentioned an allowable margin of error. This means, simply, that the point of contact is considerably larger than a pinhead. You must realize that a corner-pocket opening is about 5

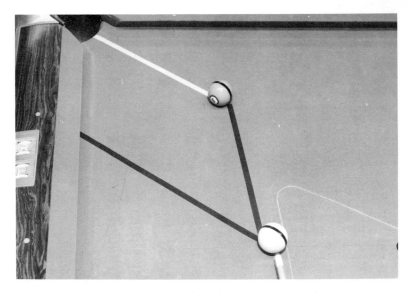

Here is the experiment in aiming described in the text. In this case, tape is used to indicate contact points both on cue and on object balls. By moving the cue ball along its intended path to where the tapes meet (lower photograph), you can illustrate to yourself what part of the cue ball you should have aimed at to make this shot.

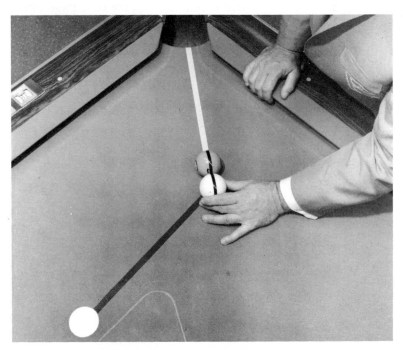

Again with tape, we illustrate that the contact point on the object ball never changes, regardless of cue-ball position.

inches wide and that object balls are $2^1/_4$ inches in diameter. In other words, you can fit two object balls in a pocket opening, and then some. Feel better? Well, don't relax too much. As the length of the shot increases, the margin for error decreases. Our game is still one of precision.

Sighting, then is a matter of determining the point of contact on an object ball. Once you have, you must retain this mental picture and prepare to send the cue ball on a path to establish contact.

Aiming: Remember our emphasis on stance in which you were positioned to bring your head directly in line with the cue? If you've ever shot a rifle, you know why.

Aiming a billiard shot is comparable to aiming a rifle in all respects except for the fact that your cheek is not against the cue as it would be against the rifle stock. There are two points of reference in aiming a billiard shot—the contact points on both cue ball and object ball. In rifle shooting, your eye follows the line from sight groove to the target.

Just beware of carrying the analogy to an extreme. The exact center of a cue ball can never be the contact point. This point always is somewhere on the curved, outside edge of the ball, and that's where your line of sight should carry to the surface point on the object ball. Only in straightaway shots—those with no angle to the pocket involved—will you be aiming across the center of the cue ball.

In answer to a frequent question about aiming, I can assure you that I always keep my eyes on the object ball during a strike. Preliminary to this, I have positioned my body and bridge hand to bring the cue tip in line with where I intend to hit the cue ball. I shift my eyes from cue ball to object ball and make any minor adjustments in

This illustration duplicates how you should visualize and aim this shot. Your line of aim should extend from the right side of the cue ball to the edge of the object ball.

Note that in aiming a shot, my head is directly above the cue and my eyes are on the object ball during the stroke.

cue position necessary, much as a golfer glances from ball to hole in putting, except that no head movement is required in billiard aiming.

From the time I start the cue back until the follow-through is completed, my eyes are glued to the object ball contact point. Then I watch the ball disappear into the pocket—most of the time.

Before I complicate things a bit, it might be well to insert a word here about confidence. Practice is the only sure foundation for successful shotmaking, and success breeds confidence. While you're practicing, think success. Golf instructors often tell their students to think of the hole as if it were a bushel basket. Remind yourself as a billiard student that the pocket is more than two balls wide and an accessible target from anywhere on the table. Self-assurance in your ability to sight, aim, and execute a variety of shots is basic to improvement.

Effects of English: In the chapter on English, I outlined in some detail the effect of right or left sideways spin on the cue ball. You

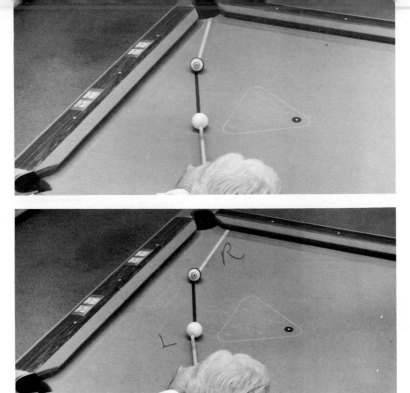

From top to bottom, we see the effect of stroking the cue ball center, English left, and English right. English left (middle photograph) throws the object ball to the right. English right (bottom photograph) throws the object ball to the left. You must compensate for this throw effect when you aim and shoot and apply English.

See pages 67 & 68

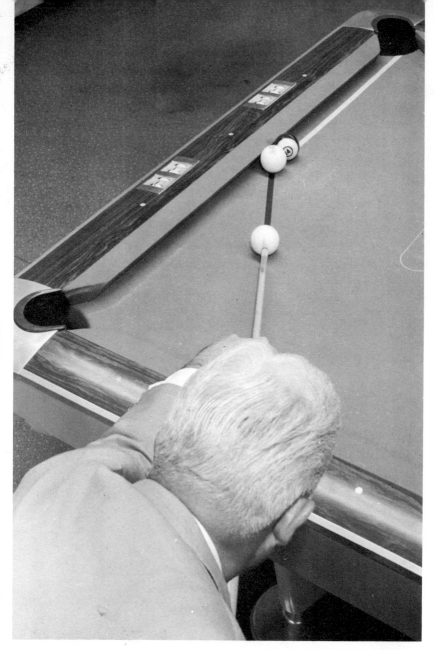

At this angle, an object ball resting against the cushion can be pocketed with a center stroke on the cue ball aimed to hit the cushion and object ball simultaneously.

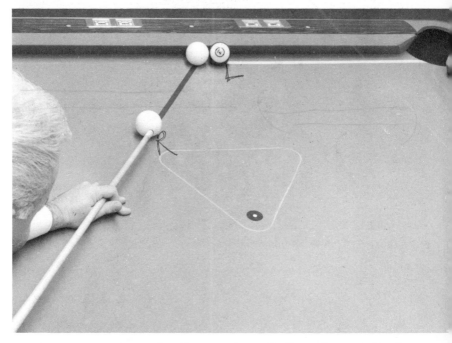

When a very thin hit is required on a cushioned ball, aim the cue ball to hit the cushion slightly behind the object ball, and apply English, in this case right-hand. This will produce a throw-left effect on the object ball, forcing it to hug the cushion on its way to the pocket.

will recall that when the cue ball is stroked to the right of center, it curves right as a result of counterclockwise spin. English left, applied by stroking the ball to the left of center, forces the ball to curve left. The amount of curve increases with the length of the shot, and a soft stroke will produce more curve than a hard one.

When a cue ball stroked for English contacts an object ball, there is a transfer of the English effect—in the opposite direction. This produces what we call a "throw" shot simply because the effect is to throw the object ball away from the direct path it would follow if it were hit by a center-stroked cue ball.

Just remember that an object ball hit with cue-ball English left will be thrown right. It would be thrown left when struck by a cue ball stroked for English right.

Throw shots are useful when you face extra-thin cuts on the

object ball and when you want the cue ball to alter its course after contact. You must compensate for the throw effect of English in aiming at the object ball. Knowing that English right on the cue ball throws the object ball left, the object-ball contact point will be further left than normal.

Here's an example of when and how to use English. When an object ball is resting against a cushion, the normal shot called for is a center-ball stroke aimed to hit cushion and ball at the same time. This keeps the object ball from bouncing away from the cushion. This standard shot at a cushioned ball will not work if the angle requires too thin a hit by the cue ball. The alternative is to drive the cue ball to the cushion slightly behind the object ball and apply English in a direction that will transfer to the object ball and force it to hug the cushion on the way to a pocket.

Combination, Carom, and Bank Shots: One of the many rewards of your increasing skill at billiards will be your ability to recognize shot opportunities where, to the less practiced eye, apparently none exist. Billiard balls have an unpredictable way of clustering in every conceivable formation. In all but a very few situations, some sort of shot possibility exists. It's up to you to muster all your sighting skill to find it.

During a championship match, I may play safe and not attempt a highly complicated shot to avoid the risk of missing and opening up the cluster for my opponent. But during your friendly games, I urge you to study the table and try for a tough shot to gain the experience.

One fascinating challenge is the combination shot, one in which two or more balls must be set in motion to drive the called ball to a pocket. It's like a chain reaction.

The common expression is to refer to a combination as "on" if it appears that a proper sequence of throw actions on intervening balls will ultimately end the called ball in the right direction. When this appears impossible, the combination is not "on."

Illustrations in this chapter show examples of combinations that are "on" and not "on."

How do you determine this business of "on" and not "on"? First,

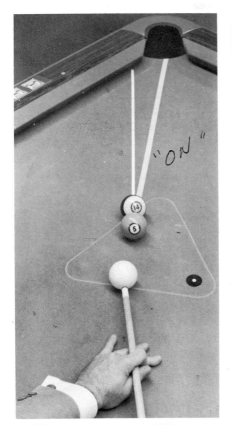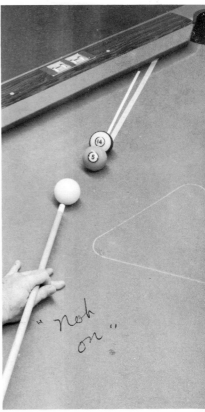

The two-ball combination at the left is "on," while the somewhat different arrangement at the right is not "on" In the "on" combination, stroke to produce the equivalent of English left on the 5-ball. This motion reverses itself in transferring to the called ball, 14, which is thrown right and into the pocket. The combination at right is not "on" because the 14-ball cannot be thrown far enough to reach the pocket.

examine the combination to make sure the balls are "frozen," or nearly so. Balls in "on" combinations must be touching or not more than one-eighth of an inch apart to sustain the transfer action. Next, determine the direction of throw required on the called ball and work back toward the cue ball to decide if the combination of throw effects on each intervening ball will result in the desired actions on the ball to be pocketed.

This is the chain reaction I mentioned in which you must use

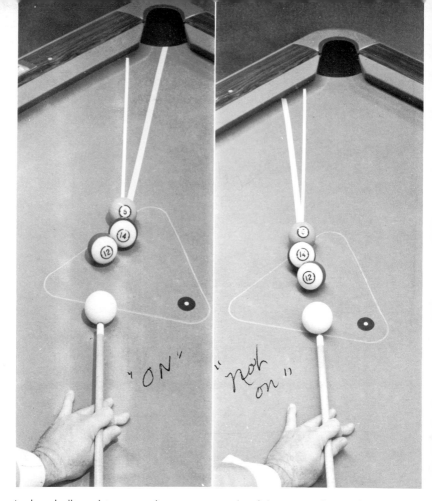

In three-ball combinations, the same principle of throw transfer applies. At the left, the shot is "on," and the 5-ball can be pocketed by throwing it to the right. A full hit on the 12-ball will start the necessary chain reaction. The combination at the right cannot be made because the called ball will be thrown left however the 12-ball is hit.

your understanding that the effect of throw reverses itself from ball to ball. When you practice, start by setting up two-ball combinations, and progress to three-, four-, and five-ball arrangements. Try shots that you are sure are "on," and arrange others that are not going to help develop your sighting sense.

Carom shots differ from combinations in that the cue ball hits a

These four-ball combinations are arranged to illustrate when the called ball can be thrown into the pocket (photograph at left) and when it cannot, as in the lineup at the right.

called ball that must deflect, or carom, off one or more other object balls to be pocketed. You can make carom shots when the balls are farther apart than is possible in combinations.

When the called ball in a carom is frozen to another object ball, an imaginary line drawn from the pocket must extend directly in between the balls to permit use of a center-ball stroke. Let's assume

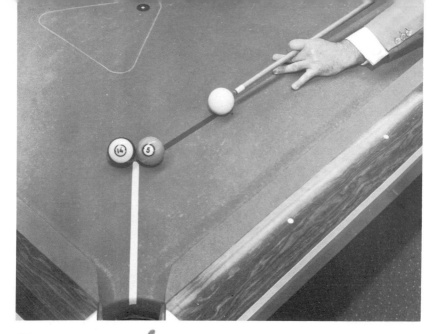

When two balls are touching, or nearly so, on this line to a pocket, call the 5-ball and hit it on the right side. It will carom off the 14, and score.

A special technique is required for this carom shot because a line from between the two balls does not extend to the pocket. To score the 5-ball, apply draw action to the cue ball. This produces overspin on the 5 and moves both balls to positions indicated by paper spots before the carom is completed.

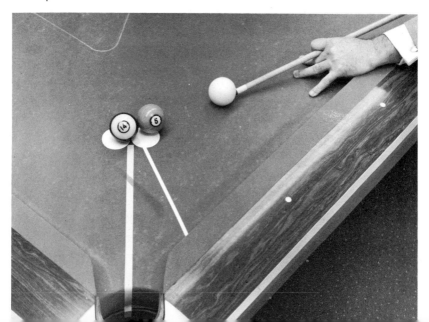

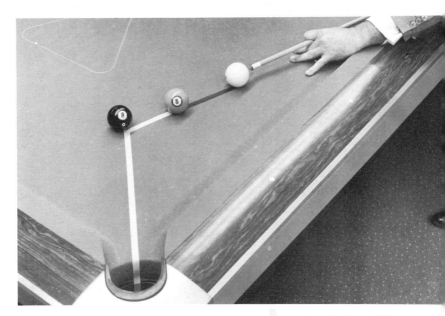

This carom shot shows the path of the 5-ball, which is made to deflect off the 8-ball and into the pocket.

the balls are frozen but not in line with a pocket. A draw shot on the cue ball will produce overspin (follow) on the called ball and force both balls toward the pocket line while the carom is taking place.

This and other carom-shot situations are illustrated here to acquaint you with a variety of carom opportunities. And here's a pleasant thought: You just might, in the process of a carom shot, pocket both the called ball and another that was carom hit. A two-point stroke like this can rarely be planned, but it's within the rules as long as the called ball is scored.

Bank shots—when an object ball strikes one or more cushions on the way to a pocket—are difficult, even for the best of players. When the house trophy is at stake, attempt a bank shot only when you're satisfied no easier shot exists and when you choose not to play safe.

A ball's reaction off the cushion is difficult to predetermine, and most bank shots must be played at the more difficult side pockets. Bank shots must be stroked harder than normal, not only because of

In this ball arrangement, the 2-ball can be made to carom off the 14- and 3-balls to give it a roundabout, but successful, path to the pocket.

the distance involved but also to keep the ball from drifting away from the proper angle as it leaves the cushion.

Bank shots are part of the game, or else it wouldn't be necessary to have more than four markers spaced along the table rails. These spots are used to determine bank-shot angles. Here's how to use them. Draw an imaginary line from the object ball to the cushion; then determine how many dot spaces this is from the pocket. Divide by two, and you have arrived at the proper bank point on the cushion. Refer to the accompanying photo for a diagram of bank-shot angles.

Remember that English affects the ball's rebound angle from a

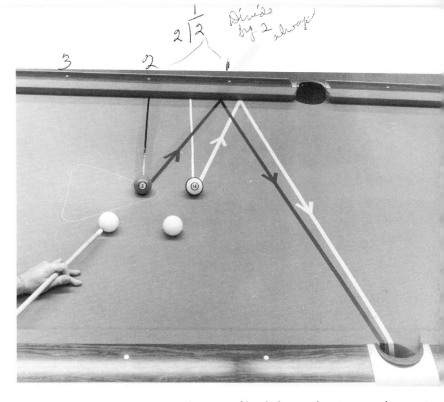

This photograph illustrates our explanation of bank-shot angles. Because the 3-ball is two rail markers above the pocket, it should be aimed through the cushion at the first marker. The 14-ball, located one and one-half markers from the pocket, must be banked halfway, or a distance three-quarters of the first marker space from the pocket.

cushion. English right on the cue ball produces what amounts to English left on the object ball. The reverse is true, of course, for English left.

There you have all you need to know—on paper at least—to sight, aim, and pocket the object ball. To really learn what you've read, play the game every chance you get. Take advantage of help from a qualified instructor, and practice, always realizing that pocket billiards is a game of judgment built on experience.

8
Sharpen Your Stroke

Practice Drills for All Players

Being close doesn't count in our game, but billiards and horse-shoes are alike in one respect—you can enjoy and learn a lot about both by playing alone. Nothing can replace the excitement of a challenging match against an opponent of equal ability, but for purposes of practice you should spend some time alone at the table, getting and keeping your stroke sharp.

In this chapter, I outline and illustrate several practice drills designed to help you progress from beginner to winner. They can take you a long way toward increasing your skill in four basic elements of billiard play:

> 1. Stroke speed
> 2. Effects of follow, draw, and English
> 3. Position play
> 4. Advanced shotmaking

Before you launch into a practice session, check your grip, stance, and bridge against the recommendations in earlier chapters. Practicing bad habits is worse than not practicing at all. I've watched too many otherwise promising players reach a certain level of skill, then falter and fail to progress further. Usually, this failing is a matter of simple faults in the player's elementary technique. For instance, too tight a grip on the cue can hinder your development of proper stroke speed and follow-through.

Now practice—often. Here are some drills for use either in practice time or as warm-ups for a match.

Start simply by spotting several balls at varying distances from side and corner pockets. Select a cue-ball spot and use center-ball stroking at each object ball. Run through a series of shots, using a

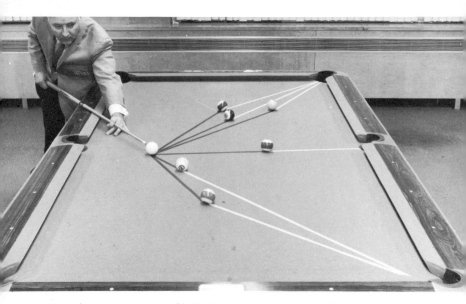

A random arrangement of balls like this provides a good warm-up exercise in center-ball stroking.

Try this series of long shots to corner pockets, using draw strokes to play position.

Playing position to pocket this series of balls clustered near a side pocket provides a test of your stroke speed.

If you can play this lineup of practice shots by controlling cue-ball movement, it means that your practice is paying off.

Using a piece of paper to indicate cue-ball position after each shot, plan a run of balls leading to good break position. A follow stroke here will send the cue ball to the rail and out.

basic bridge, then move the cue-ball spot closer to the cushion and re-shoot the series, using a rail bridge.

Try Long Shots: Bothered by the difficulty of long shots? You're not alone, and that's why even professional players try to avoid scattering the balls over the full length of the table. At times, long shots will be unavoidable, and when you face them, come equipped with experience gained in practice. Spot object balls near each corner pocket and play them the long way. Follow this drill by spotting several balls along the head string, and shoot for the corner pockets at the foot rail.

You can put your draw-shot skill to a test with this one. Arrange a semicircle of balls near a side pocket. Start at either end and work your way left or right, pocketing a ball and drawing your cue ball back into position for the next shot. Stroke speed, as well as draw action, will be practiced in this setup.

Now angle four balls or more down the length of the table, with the ball nearest you closer to the cushion. With the cue ball along

A stop shot here pockets the object ball, which occupies position in the rack area, and leaves the cue ball in line for a side-pocket shot.

Another stop shot here provides good cue-ball position to score the key ball.

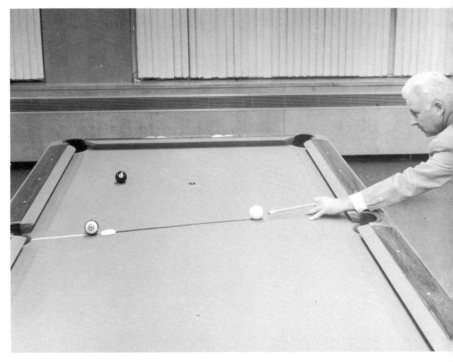

Again a stop shot is called for to pocket the key ball and position the cue ball at an angle that makes the break shot relatively easy.

the head string, stroke your way up the table with the idea in mind of playing the best possible cue-ball position for the succeeding shot.

Position Drill: To attain even more precision in playing position, use a piece of paper as a training device. Scatter a few balls on the table—I would advise less than the full 15 to avoid blocking pockets—and start calling your shots, two at a time. Before you shoot, spot the piece of paper at the desired cue-ball position for the next shot. You will be aiming both to pocket a ball and to bring the cue ball to rest on or near the paper.

While you're at it, go ahead and rack the balls for a game of 14.1 Continuous or Rotation Billiards. Play yourself a match, but don't

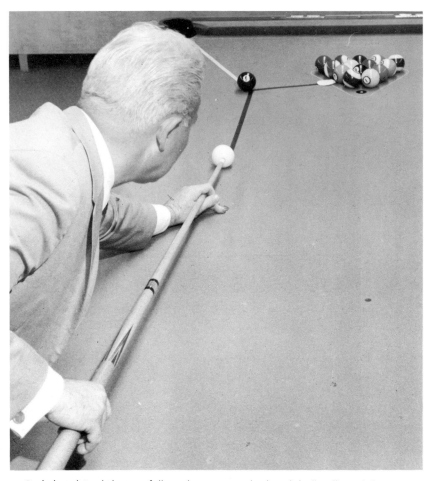

Right-hand English on a follow shot against the break ball will send the cue ball into the rack and scatter the object balls sufficiently to keep your run intact.

pull any shady stuff because you'll be watching. On second thought, why not reset the shots you miss and try again? It's only practice.

Now that you are flushed with victory in a match against yourself, set up a few combination and carom shots like those illustrated in the previous chapter. Contrary to the old adage, practice won't make you perfect. But it will bring you as close to perfection as ambition and talent will permit. And it's enjoyable.

9
Let's Play the Game

How to Win at 14.1 Pocket Billiards

As Shakespeare had Cleopatra say to one of her attendants, "Let's to billiards."

Having learned your lessons well, it is time now to tackle a game of 14.1 Continuous-Play Pocket Billiards. That's the full title of the game of 14.1, which is the common form of tournament and league competition. It is a demanding challenge of all the skills in pocket billiards, combining the strategy of offense and defense.

The term "14.1 Continuous Play" describes game procedure. Starting with the full rack of 15 balls, a player stays at the table until he misses. Balls are pocketed until one remains. The 14 pocketed balls then are reracked, and the game proceeds until one player reaches a predetermined point total, usually 125 or 150.

A digest of rules for 14.1 and other pocket-billiards games is printed elsewhere in this book. We shall discuss some of the rules here as they apply to the situations we outline.

Play to Win: On offense, your goal is to stay at the table as long as possible to build a "run" of successive points before you miss or purposely let your opponent take over as a defensive maneuver. Concentration on the following basic elements of offense can make you a winner:

—Play cue-ball position. This means controlling the cue ball so that it comes to rest at a spot you have determined best for the next shot. You should keep the cue ball away from the cushions. A cushioned cue ball limits your choice of stroke.

—Avoid long shots. This is another way of urging you to stroke soft, with just enough force to pocket the object ball and position the cue ball. Excessive stroke force can scatter object balls the full length of the table, creating more difficult shots. Top players attempt to confine their shots to the upper half of the table from side pockets to foot rail.

—Break apart object-ball clusters. Part of your position play should involve spreading apart object balls that are clustered, and clearing the paths to pockets.

—Plan ahead. Keeping a run intact and assuring yourself of a good break shot against a new rack calls for planning shots well in advance. When you step to the table, survey the arrangement of balls to determine the best sequence of shots leading to the break.

How the Game Starts: Players "lag" to start a game. In the lag, each player shoots a cue ball from behind the head string to the foot rail and back to the head rail. The player whose ball rests closest to the head rail has the option of shooting first or forcing his opponent to do so.

The lag winner usually elects to have his opponent shoot first because it is unlikely that an object ball can be pocketed in a break shot against the 15-ball rack. In turn, the player who must shoot first usually plays safe on an opening break. To accomplish this without a two-point penalty, he must hit the rack of balls, driving two object balls and the cue ball to a cushion. Since playing safe on the opening is common strategy, it is worth practicing.

A standard form of opening break shot is illustrated in this chapter. With the cue ball "in hand," meaning I can position it anywhere behind the head string, I stroke for a thin hit on one of the corner balls in the rack. The cue ball and the opposite corner ball are forced to separate cushions and return to near their original position in the rack. The cue ball strikes three cushions and comes to rest near the head rail.

Since no ball was pocketed, my opponent takes over with his chances to score about as slim as mine were as the first shooter. Had I failed to send two object balls and the cue ball to a cushion, I

Opposite page, bottom:
Playing a safety requires hitting an object ball and driving it, or the cue ball, to a cushion. In this safety, I hit the corner ball very thin to avoid disturbing the rack, and return the cue ball to the head end of the table.

My favorite opening break shot produces a thin hit on a corner ball, sending it and the opposite corner ball to different cushions and back to the rack. The cue ball hits three cushions and comes to rest near the head rail. Executed properly, this break shot will force your opponent to play a safety.

In playing this safety, I bank the cue ball off two cushions before it touches an object ball on its return path to the head rail.

would have been handed the two-point penalty and perhaps been forced to break again at my opponent's option.

Because my break shot was successful, my opponent can either shoot away by calling the ball he intends to pocket, or announce his intention to play a safety.

Safety Play: Safety play in billiards is like a football coach substituting his heavyweight linemen for a goal-line stand. Both are designed to keep opponents from scoring.

To execute a safety without a penalty, a player must drive an object ball to a cushion or drive the cue ball to a cushion after contact with an object ball. Failure at either alternative results in a scratch and a one-point penalty. You should play a safety anytime the object ball arrangement is such that no reasonable shot exists. Attempting, and missing, an extremely difficult shot can open up

Another safety sends a corner ball to the cushion and back to the ball cluster, while the cue ball comes to rest near the foot rail.

the balls and permit your opponent to shoot away with ease.

Illustrated here are several safety shots in which the balls were disturbed very little and the cue ball was returned to a position difficult for my opponent. This is the purpose of safety play. If I am forced to relinquish the table, I want my opponent to face a shot situation as tough as the one he left me.

Scratch Play: During the course of play in a tight match, a situation could develop in which you might intentionally stroke to relinquish the table and accept a one-point penalty. This is called "playing a scratch." To do so, you need only stroke the cue ball and intentionally fail to meet the requirements for a safety.

Unintentional scratches, when the cue ball enters a pocket or jumps off the table, also result in a one-point penalty, and give your opponent the next shot with the cue ball "in hand." Any object ball

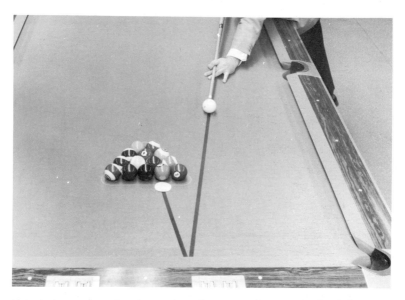

Here I play an intentional scratch and accept a 1-point penalty. I chose not to risk disturbing the pack, and banked the cue ball to the cluster, which will force my opponent also to play a defensive shot.

pocketed during a scratch is respotted on the table and is not scored.

Just beware of scratching, unintentionally or accidentally, on three successive turns at the table. Three scratches, without an intervening point scored or safety, result in a 15-point penalty.

Play Position: Once the balls are spread sufficiently to permit shooting away, perhaps after a series of safeties, you can proceed to plan and execute a sequence of shots. Sight carefully to pocket an object ball, and move the cue ball with the follow, draw, or English action necessary to position it for the next shot. Remember the requirement to call your shots. You must announce to your opponent, or the referee, the number of the ball you intend to score and the pocket it will reach.

As you progress through a series of shots, you should be looking ahead to both the "key" ball and the "break" ball.

The key ball will be the next-to-last ball remaining on the table after pocketing the others. It is key because in scoring it you must

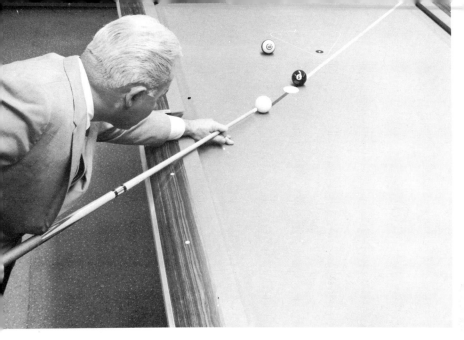

Playing the key ball to produce the best possible cue-ball position for the break is vital to extending a run. A stop shot (top photograph) or a follow shot (lower photograph) is necessary in these break-ball situations.

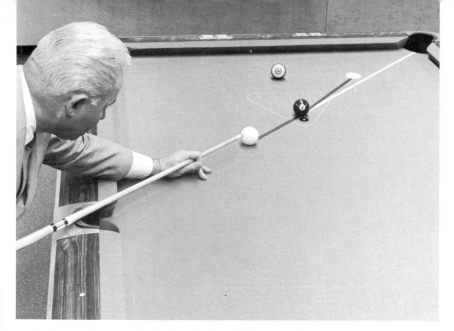

In the top photograph, the key ball is pocketed from within the rack area, and follow action on the cue ball sends it to good break position. Draw action is required in the lower photograph to draw the cue ball back from the key ball and into an easy angle for the break shot.

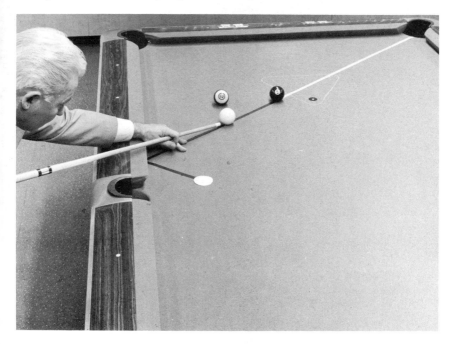

attempt to send the cue ball to a position from where it will be possible both to score the break ball and scatter a new rack of 14 object balls.

Break Shot: To maintain a run of more than 14 balls—and practice will make this possible—you must pocket the break ball and drive the cue ball into the new rack with force sufficient to spread apart the cluster. While it's possible to scatter the rack from practically any break-ball and cue-ball position on the table, obviously some positions are better than others.

It's up to you in planning your shots to save as your break ball the one that appears best positioned for this purpose in relation to your intended cue-ball spot after pocketing the key ball. You will note in

Employ follow with English left in this break shot to a wide pocket. This shot is somewhat difficult because of the force required to send the cue ball to two cushions before it hits the racked balls.

When object balls must be respotted, they must be placed on the foot spot. If the spot is blocked by another object ball, as it is here, the ball to be respotted must be placed behind the blocking ball and on a straight line from foot spot to foot rail.

This and the following seven photographs show break shots from various break-ball and cue-ball positions. Follow action on the cue ball here will send it into the pack.

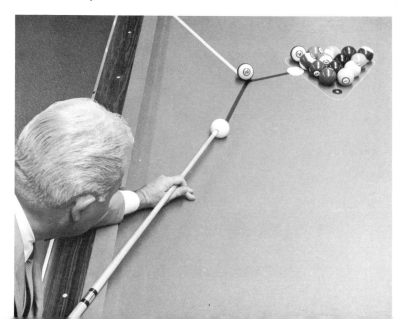

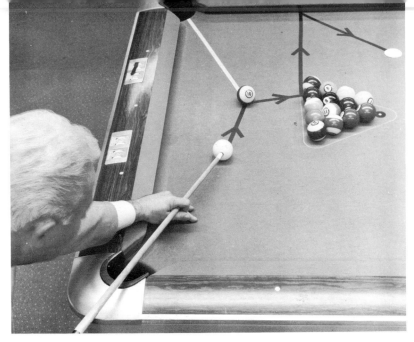

A follow shot with English right is necessary in this break-shot situation.

English left with follow against the break ball here will drive the cue ball into the pack and then away from the scattering balls.

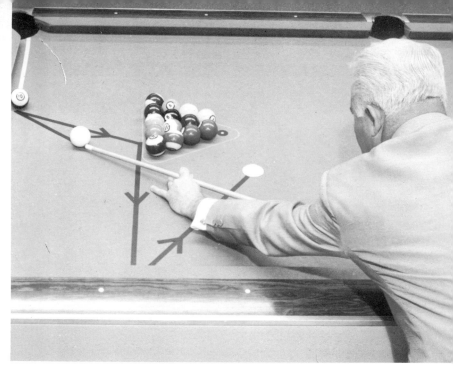

Sharp draw action on the cue ball is required to pull it into the rack with enough force to open up the cluster.

Banking the cue ball after a thin hit on the break ball can open the cluster in this situation.

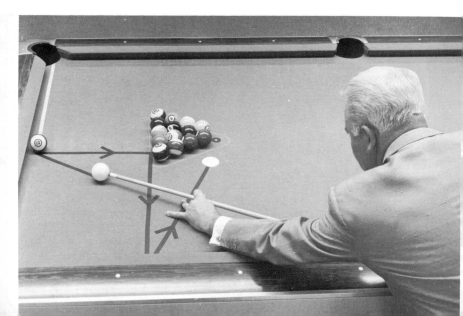

Follow with English left can open the rack from this difficult break-shot position.

English right will force the cue ball into the rack and then to a cushion while the balls separate.

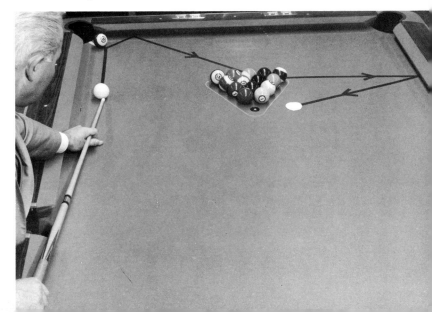

the illustrations that a pencil line is drawn around the ball-racking triangle to play 14.1. This is necessary to give the players an area of reference for selection of a break-ball and cue-ball position for the break.

If the final unpocketed ball is within the rack area, it must be placed on the head spot to permit the reracking of the other 14 balls. When both the cue ball and the final unpocketed ball interfere with the rack, all 15 object balls are racked, and the player must shoot the cue ball from behind the head string.

When only the cue ball interferes with the rack, and the final object ball is above the head string, the 14 balls are racked as usual and the cue ball is "in hand" to be shot from behind the head string. In this situation, if the object ball is behind the head string, the cue ball must be shot from the head spot.

Now, play the game and may all your runs be long ones.

10
Just for Fun

Learn to Perform Trick Shots

Try this for a bit of home-style heroics. The next time you stroll into a billiard center or invite the neighbors to your home for a game, spot six balls in a cluster near the center of the table. Then, with as much nonchalance as you can muster, drive the cue ball into the cluster and relish the "oh's" and "ah's" from your spectators when each of the six balls plops home in a different pocket.

Sound impossible? Well, let me assure you it isn't. Any player of average ability who is willing to practice can learn to perform all the trick shots diagrammed in this chapter—and many more.

I enjoy entertaining people by setting up and making a series of seemingly impossible shots. And it's always a highlight to select an unlikely shooter from the crowd and let him or her successfully make the shot I have arranged.

This illustrates the fact that ball placement is far more important than the stroke in a trick shot.

The late Charlie Peterson compiled what must have been the greatest repertoire of trick shots by challenging his audiences, "Show me a shot I can't make." To my knowledge, no one ever could.

I don't pretend to follow in Charlie's trick-shot footsteps. His sincere boast does point up the infinite variety of trick-shot possibilities, and for you, this means unlimited enjoyment. Some trial-and-error practice is required to master the shots described here and others you may develop. Be a trick-shot hero. That's part of the fun of our game.

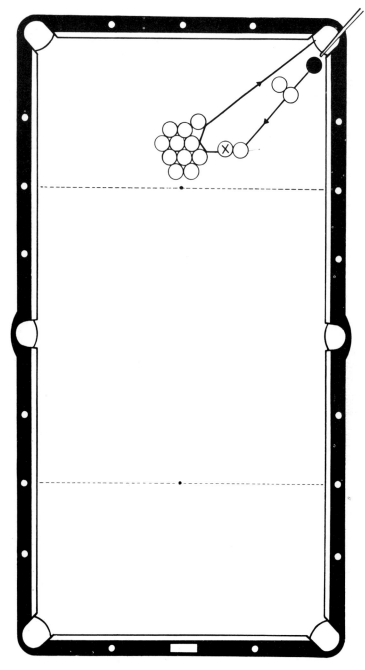

"THE HUSTLER": Here's a shot I arranged for Jackie Gleason to make in the motion picture *The Hustler*. A center stroke on the blocked cue ball will set three balls in motion, forcing the called ball into a carom back to the upper right corner pocket.

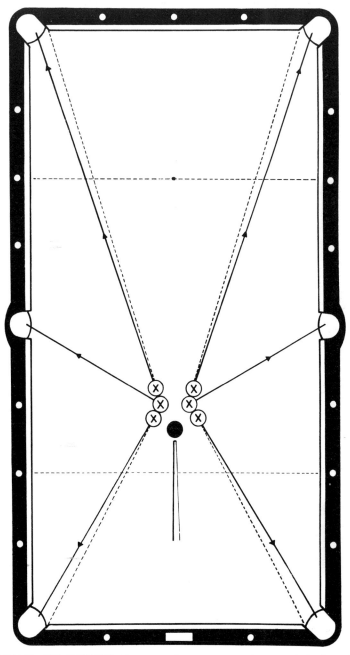

SIX BALLS—SIX POCKETS: The secret here is to aim the outside balls to the inside edge of the corner pockets as indicated by the dotted lines. Strike the cue ball (in back) hard and slightly below center.

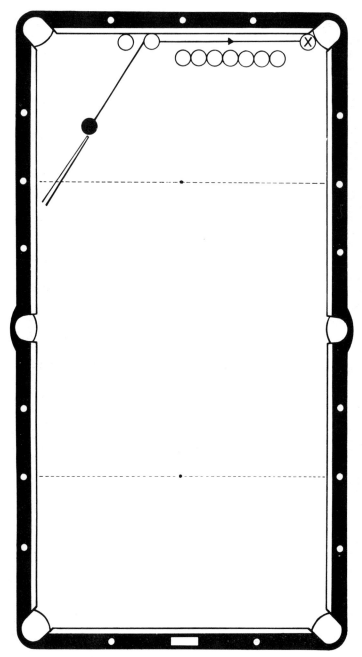

MACHINE GUN: Place the long string of balls in a line slightly less than a ball's width from the cushions. Strike the cue ball with high right English to force the struck object ball along the cushion. It will produce a "chatter" sound as it touches each ball in the lineup before pocketing the called ball, marked with an X.

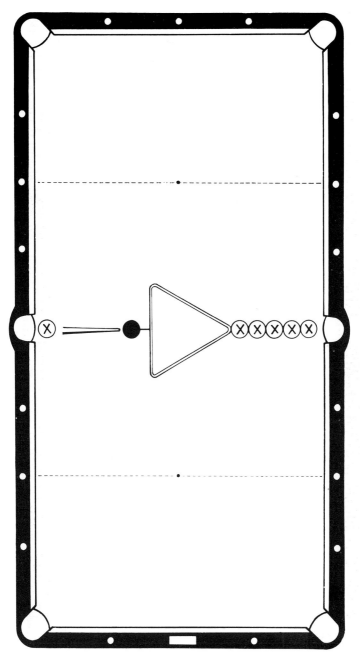

SIX BALLS—TWO POCKETS: Strike the cue ball with extreme draw. This will pull back the cue ball to pocket the single object ball after pushing the triangle against the other five, forcing them into the other side pocket.

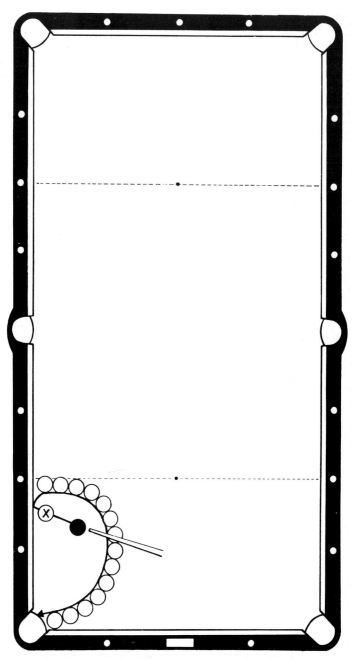

AROUND THE RING: A center-ball shot here will break the called ball off the cushion and into the corner pocket after it contacts each of the object balls sent in a semicircle.

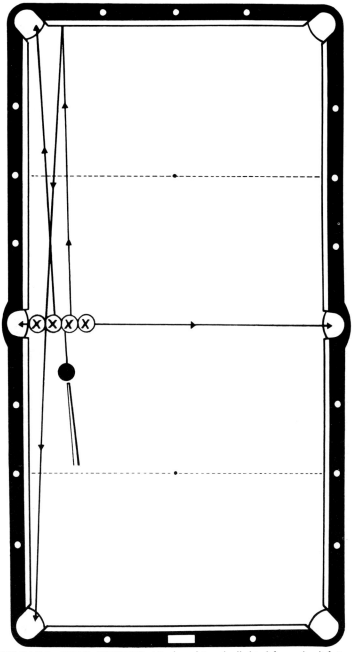

FOUR BALLS—FOUR POCKETS: Hit the object ball third from the left in this setup on the left side with a draw stroke on the cue ball. This keeps the cue ball out of the path of the third ball as it returns from the foot rail to the lower left corner pocket.

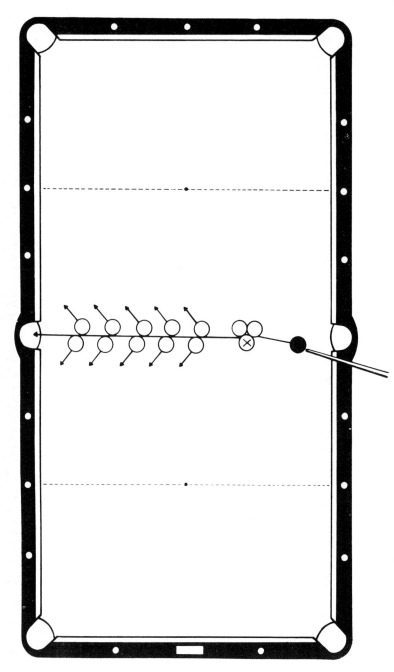

FOOTBALL SHOT: High left English on the cue ball in this arrangement will send the lower-right ball in the three-ball cluster through the 10-ball lineup like a "blocker" opening the path for the called ball.

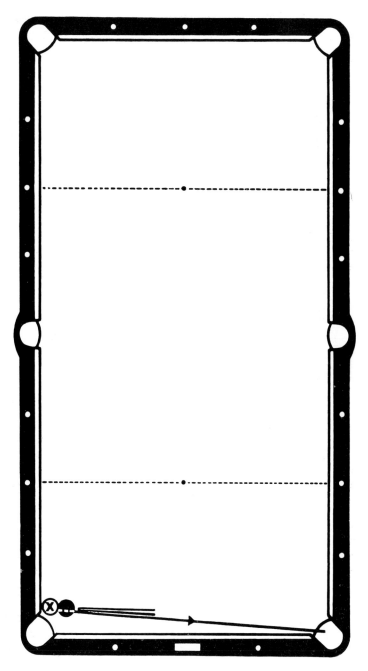

SHARP BANK: Hit the cue ball sharply above center (follow stroke) to force the called ball off the cushion and into the opposite corner pocket. The cue must be lifted quickly after the stroke to avoid interfering with the banked ball.

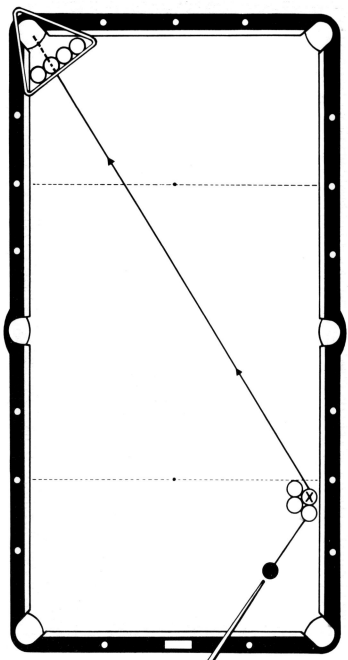

JUMP THE RACK: A center hit on the cue ball against this cluster will send the called ball off the cushion and into the corner pocket by hitting the edge of the rack and jumping over the row of four balls. The rack must be wedged upright against the cushion.

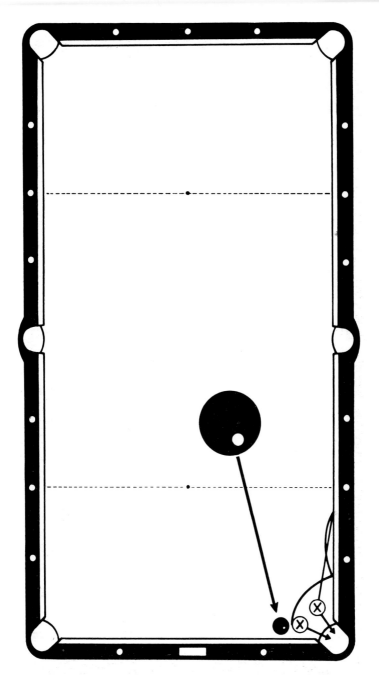

SHORT MASSE: Strike the cue ball at the spot indicated in the enlarged view to produce radical backspin. The cue ball can be made to follow the black-line path to pocket both object balls. A word of warning: Missing the cue ball on this stroke can rip the cloth of the table.

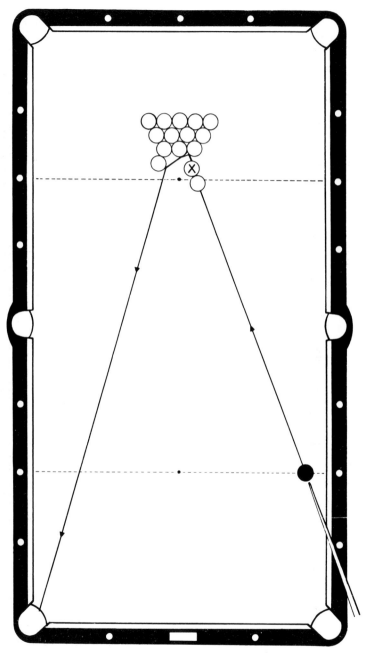

HANDKERCHIEF SHOT: Cover this ball arrangement with a handkerchief to make it look more difficult. A sharp center stroke on the cue ball will carom the called ball off three others in the pack and into the lower left corner pocket.

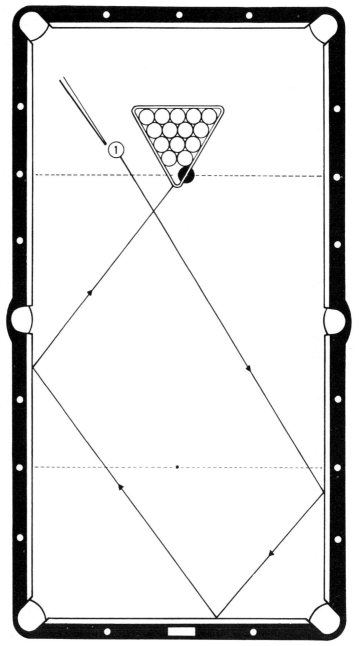

LAZY MAN'S RACK: Apply high right English to the 1-ball, and bank it off three cushions toward the foot spot. The ball will shove aside the cue ball on which the rack is resting, permitting the rack to drop to the table.

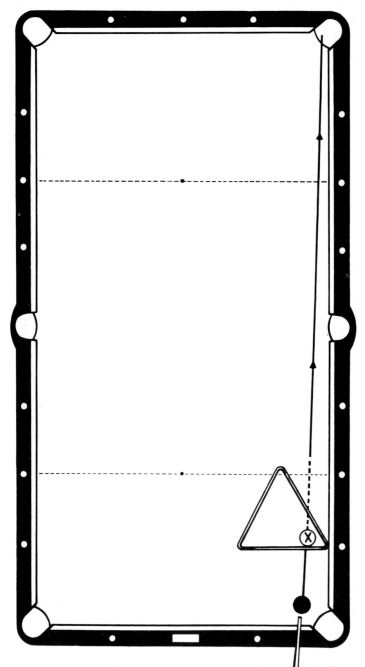

JUMP OUT: Elevate the butt end of the cue and strike the cue ball sharply above center. The cue ball can be made to jump over the edge of the rack, forcing the called ball to jump over the opposite edge of the rack and travel to the upper right corner pocket.

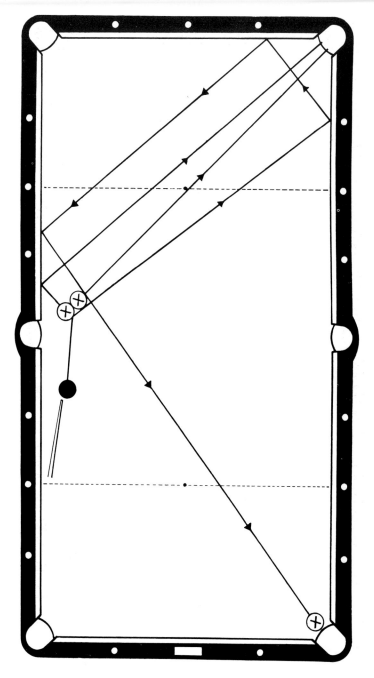

THREE IN ONE: High left English on the cue ball will drive two object balls to the upper right corner pocket. The cue ball then continues to bank off three cushions and return to pocket the third object ball positioned at the lower right corner pocket.

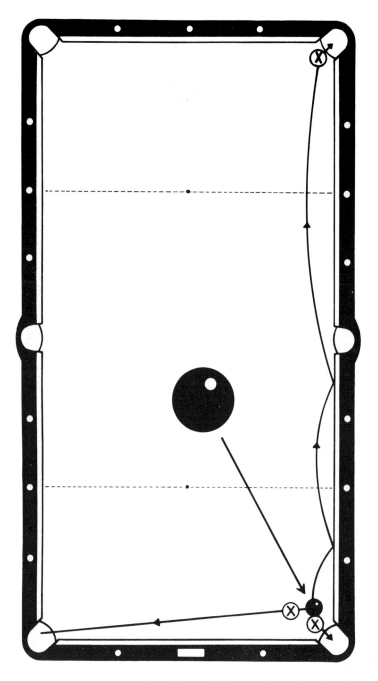

LONG MASSE: A massé stroke at the cue-ball spot indicated in the enlarged view can be made to pocket both balls at the head end of the table and travel along the side rail to pocket the ball at the upper right corner pocket.

BLOCKED CUE BALL: With the cue ball blocked behind the pocket opening, use a center stroke to bank off the side rail and into the cluster. The called ball, positioned as it is here, will carom into the upper right corner pocket.

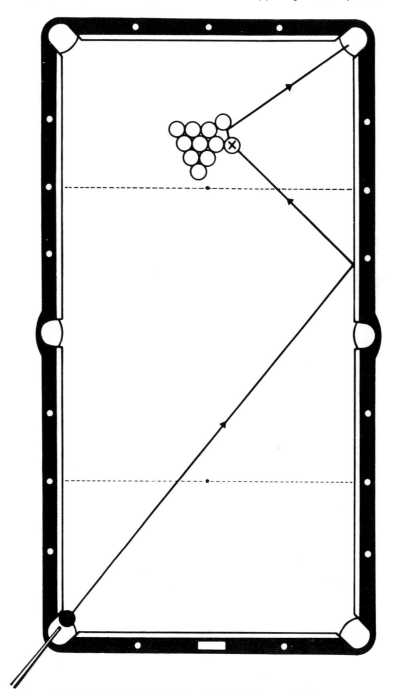

UNDER THE BRIDGE: Position the mechanical bridge, two object balls, and the cue ball as shown here. Elevate the butt end of the cue and strike the cue ball sharply for a draw shot. This drives one object ball under the bridge to a pocket, and forces the cue ball to jump over the bridge and return to pocket the second object ball.

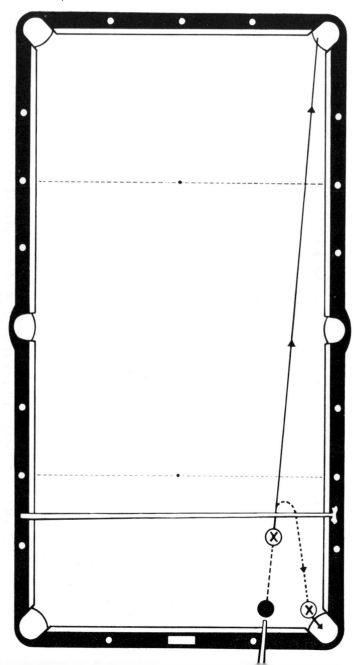

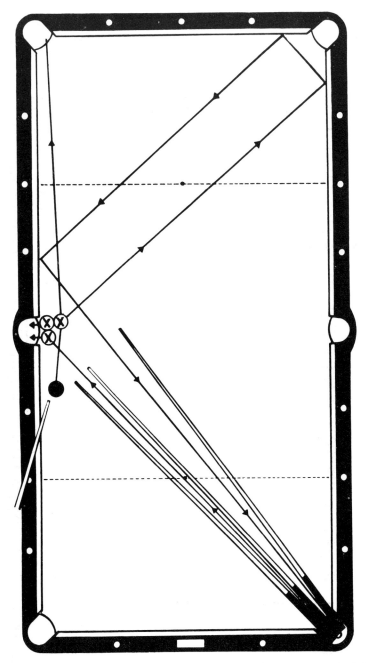

RAILROAD SHOT: Wedge three cues into a pocket for this shot. A high left-English stroke on the cue ball will drive two object balls to separate pockets and send the cue ball to three cushions before it travels up and down the cues to pocket the third object ball.

11
Talk a Good Game

Glossary of Terms and Expressions

Billiards is an ancient sport, and through the centuries players have coined a collection of colorful terms to describe rules and situations of play. Much of the common vernacular of pocket billiards is given here in the hope that it will help increase your knowledge and appreciation of the game.

ANGLED. When the corner of a pocket prevents the player from shooting the cue ball in a straight line at an object ball.

BALL ON. When it can be shot at in a straight line or can be drven into a called pocket on a combination or carom shot.

BALLS STRUCK SIMULTANEOUSLY. It is permissible to strike balls simultaneously in call-shot pocket billiards if the player calls both ball and pocket.

BANK SHOT. Results when a player drives an object ball against a cushion and then into a pocket from that cushion.

BREAK. Opening shot of the game.

BRIDGE. The hand position as it holds and guides the cue shaft. It is also short for a mechanical bridge, a device used to make shots the player otherwise could not reach.

CALL SHOT. A requirement of some games that the player must make known his object ball and pocket intention before he shoots.

CALLED BALL. The ball a player announces he intends to score in a called pocket.

CALLED POCKET. The pocket into which a player announces he intends to drop a called ball.

CAROM. A shot in which the cue ball strikes each of two object balls; a rebounding, especially at an angle. *See also* KISS.

COMBINATION SHOT. A shot in which the cue ball sets in motion one or more intervening balls, with the last one striking the called object ball. A "chain reaction."

COUNT. A score—a point or number of points. In rotation, the number value of the ball pocketed.

CUE BALL IN HAND. When the player puts the ball in play at a point of his choice within the head string *(q.v.)*.

CUSHION. The cloth-covered rubber ridge that borders the inside rails of the table.

CUT. To hit an object ball less than full at the center, causing the ball to deflect at an angle.

DEAD BALL. One that stops upon contact, the result of a stop shot.

DRAW. A stroking technique that allows the player to draw the cue ball back from an object ball.

ENGLISH. A stroking influence to control the action of the cue ball either before or after it hits an object ball. The result of ball spin.

FANCY SHOT. Usually an exhibition shot, a shot that requires unusual skill; a trick shot.

FEATHERING. To hit an object ball very thinly.

FOLLOW. A stroking technique that makes the cue ball roll in the same general direction as the struck object ball. Opposite of "draw."

FOOT SPOT. The spot for placement of object balls at the start of most games.

FORCE. The speed applied to the cue ball.

FORCE DRAW. The powerful application of "draw" to the cue ball, forcing the cue ball "through" the object ball before the cue ball begins to draw back, or drawing the cue ball back a great distance from the object ball.

FORCE FOLLOW. The firm application of follow that can drive the cue ball in a straight line "through" the object ball to a desired position.

FOUL. An infraction of game rules. It is penalized by loss of points.

FOUL STROKE. A rules infraction in which the foul takes place as a result of a player's stroke. Example: double contact of the cue tip with the cue ball.

FROZEN. Used to describe balls that are touching each other. When object balls are frozen, they remain in play. When the cue ball is frozen to an object, the player proceeds according to the rules of the game being played. A ball resting against a cushion is also said to be frozen.

FULL BALL. The contact of the cue ball with an object ball at its exact center—as opposed to a ball "cut" one-half, one-third, and so on.

HEAD OF TABLE. The short rail marked by the manufacturer's nameplate.

HEAD SPOT. A spot at the midpoint of a line drawn from the side-rail second diamonds of the side rails near the head of the table.

HEAD STRING. A line through the head spot. Most games of pocket billiards start with a break shot from behind this line.

HIGH RUN. The highest consecutive series of scored balls in one inning of a game or tournament.

HOLD. Similar to stop or draw action applied to the ball. Any action applied to hold the cue ball back from the course it would normally take.

HUG THE RAIL. When action on the cue ball forces it to roll along or bounce several times against the rail.

INNING. A turn at the table, terminated when a player misses, fouls, scores the maximum number of balls allowed, or ends the game.

KISS. A carom. The cue ball may kiss from one object ball to another. A struck object ball may kiss one or more other object balls.

LAGGING. To determine rotation of play, each player shoots a cue ball from behind the head string to the foot rail and back to the head rail. The player whose ball rests closest to the head rail has the option of shooting first.

LIVE BALL. A ball that is in play under the rules. Also, the cue ball, when its action is "alive" rather than "dead." *See* DEAD BALL.

LONG STRING. An imaginary line drawn for tournament play, from the foot spot to the center of the foot rail, on which balls are spotted when the foot spot is occupied.

MASSE. Extreme application of English on the cue ball, accomplished by elevating the cue to nearly perpendicular.

MISCUE. Faulty contact of the cue tip with the cue ball, caused by the tip slipping off its intended point of contact. It is also caused by a defective tip, improper chalking, or a player's unsuccessful attempt to apply excessive English.

MISS. Failure of a player to accomplish his intention on a stroke. Ends an inning and may or may not be a foul, depending on the rules of the game.

NATURAL. A simple shot.

PACK. A cluster of balls at the foot spot either before or after a break shot.

PUSH SHOT. Shoving the cue ball with the tip of the cue, or two contacts of the cue tip on the cue ball. Push shots are legal if the stroke is made with what appears to be one continuous motion. The referee is the sole judge of push-shot legality.

PYRAMID. The placement of object balls in a triangle at the foot spot to start a game.

RACK. The triangular equipment used to arrange object balls in pyramid form at the foot spot to start a game. It also describes the arrangement of object balls after the triangle is removed.

REVERSE. English applied to put "hold" on the ball. It also describes English left, the opposite of "natural," or English right.

ROTATION. The name of a game in which the player must shoot at object balls in numerical order.

RUN. A series of consecutive scores in one inning.

SAFETY. A defensive maneuver that is accomplished when a player sacrifices his opportunity to score, plays "safe" under the rules, ends his turn, and attempts to leave a difficult shot for his opponent.

SCRATCH. Unanticipated development in a stroke that may or may not be a foul, depending on game rules. Pocketing the cue ball is a scratch. Failure to meet specifications of a safety shot also is a scratch.

SETUP. An easy shot.

SNOOKERED. To be unable to shoot the cue ball directly at an object ball.

SPOT BALL. A ball that is placed at the foot, center, or head spot to conform with a rule of play.

SPOT SHOT. When a player shoots at a ball that has been placed on a spot.

SPOTTING. The replacement of balls on the table as required by the rules of the game.

V-BRIDGE. Used when the bridge must be elevated to shoot over intervening balls.

12
Know the Rules

Digest of Regulations

Here is a simplified version of rules for various pocket-billiards games, including 14.1 Continuous Play, the accepted form of league and championship tournament competition. Complete rules are published by the Billiard Congress of America, the official sanctioning and rules-making organization in the game.

14.1 Continuous Play

RACK. The balls are racked on the foot spot with the higher-numbered balls placed in the foot-spot apex of the triangle. Numerical order is not required. A pencil line is drawn around the triangle.

OPENING BREAK. Players lag for break. The player winning the lag has the option of breaking or of forcing his opponent to do so. The starting player must drive two object balls and the cue ball to a cushion, or pocket a called object ball. The penalty for failure to meet these requirements is two points, and the opposing player has the option of accepting the shot or of forcing another break. If two object balls are driven to a cushion and the cue ball is pocketed (scratched), the penalty is one point, and the incoming player has the cue ball "in hand" to shoot from behind the head string.

SCORING. To score, a player must pocket the object ball after indicating that ball by number and the pocket in which it will fall. Any additional balls pocketed on the same stroke are also scored. A player continues at the table until he misses, fouls, plays a safety, or scratches. The first player to reach 150 wins the game or block, if

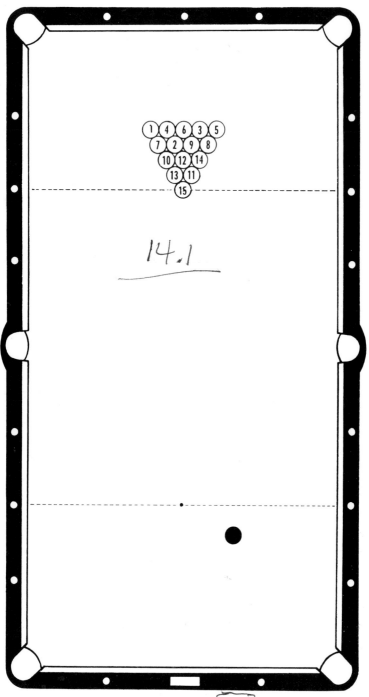

14.1

Opening Rack for 14.1

several blocks of 150 form a match. (There are exceptions to the 150-point game total, particularly in league play. For example, some league rules may limit the number of balls a player may run, perhaps 14, and the number of innings, perhaps 20, for a game total of 280.)

SAFETY PLAY. A player is not obligated to announce his intention to play a safety. Playing a safety requires a player to drive an object ball to a cushion or to drive the cue ball to a cushion after contact with an object ball. Failure to meet the requirements of a safety is termed a scratch, and the penalty is one point.

SCRATCH. A player is charged with a scratch, and the loss of one point, when he fails to meet the requirements of a safety or when the cue ball is pocketed. The penalty for each scratch is one point, but an additional penalty of 15 points is assessed when a player strokes three successive scratches.

PENALTIES. The following is a summary of situations requiring a penalty—the loss of a point or points:

1. Failure to meet opening-break requirements, two points.
2. Shoving the cue ball or touching it with anything but the cue tip, such as the side of the cue or clothing, one point.
3. Playing a scratch, one point.
4. Not having at least one foot touching the floor during a stroke, one point.
5. Stroking while the cue ball or object ball is in motion, one point.
6. Playing three successive scratches, 15 points.

JUMPED BALLS. When the cue ball jumps off the table, the player loses the inning, is penalized one point, and the stroke is termed a scratch. If a called object ball jumps the table, it is respotted, and the player loses the inning without penalty. When a single stroke results in pocketing a called ball and sending another object ball off the table, the jumped ball is respotted and the player continues.

Rotation

RACK. The balls are racked with the 1-ball on the foot spot, the 2-ball at the left corner, and the 3-ball at the right corner of the full rack, and the 15-ball in the center.

OPENING BREAK. The players lag for break. The 1-ball is the first object ball. It must be pocketed, or another ball pocketed after cue-ball contact with the 1-ball, or the break-shot player loses the inning.

SCORING. The lowest-numbered ball on the table is the object ball. It must be struck first; otherwise it or any other ball pocketed on the same stroke cannot be scored. All illegally pocketed balls are respotted. The number of a ball is its score value. The game ends when one player or a side reaches 61 points.

Eight Ball

RACK. The balls are racked at the foot spot, with the 8-ball at the center of the rack, a stripe ball in one corner of the rack, and a solid ball in the other corner.

OPENING BREAK. The players lag for break. The beginning player need not call a ball on the break. If he does not score, he loses the inning. If he pockets a ball, its number determines his set of future object balls 1 through 7 (solid), or 9 through 15 (stripes).

SCORING. A player remains at the table until he misses pocketing a ball in his set. If a ball is not scored in the pocket specified, it must be respotted. After a player pockets all the balls in his set, he must score the 8-ball in a called pocket to win. He loses the game if he pockets the 8-ball before pocketing his set or if he fails to drive the cue ball or the 8-ball to a cushion when shooting to score it.

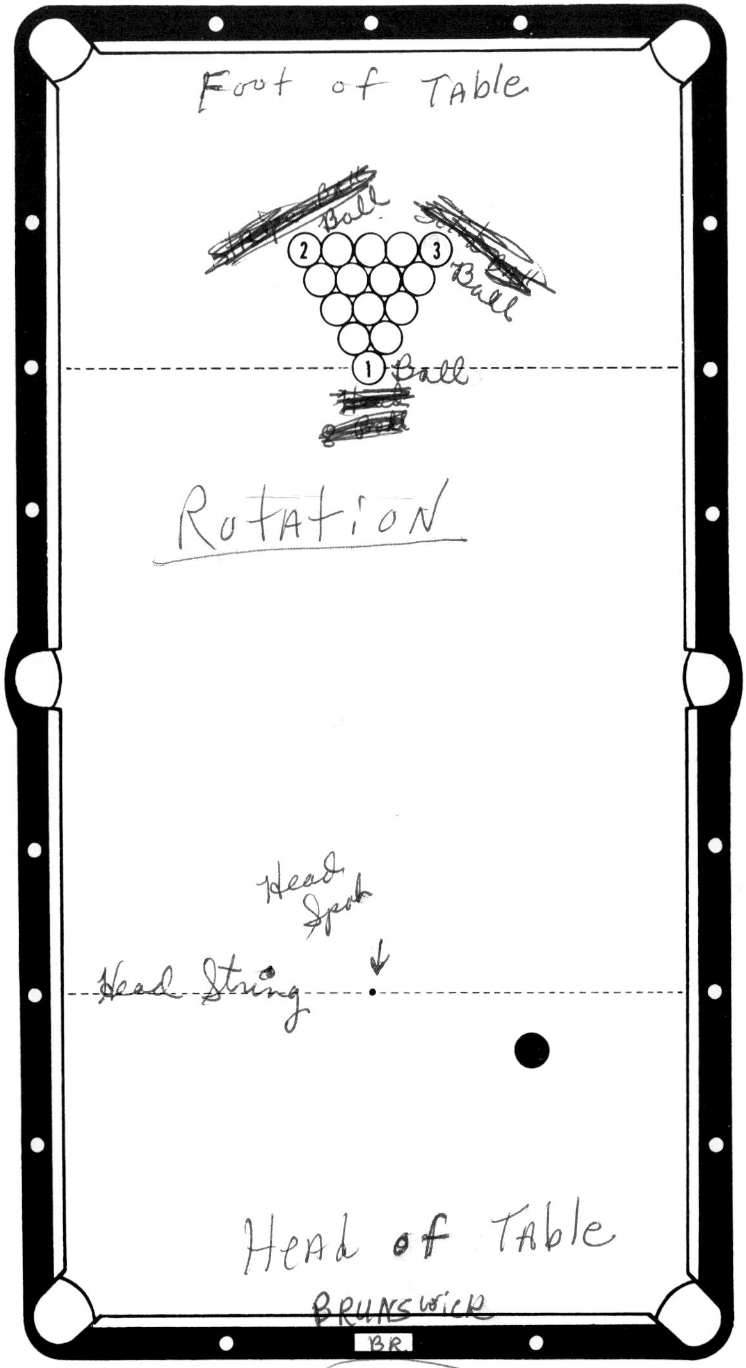

Foot of Table

Ball

2 3

Ball

1 Ball

Rotation

Head Spot

Head String

Head of Table

BRUNSWICK

BR.

Balls Racked for Rotation

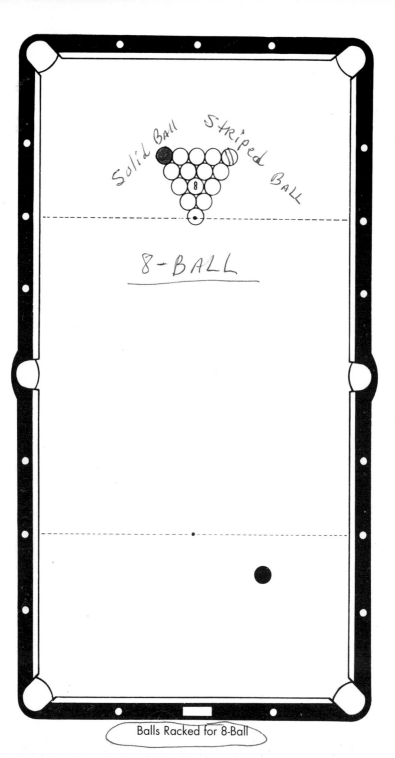

Solid Ball   Striped Ball

8-BALL

Balls Racked for 8-Ball